CONSECRATED GROUND

GEORGE BOYD

TALONBOOKS

Talonbooks
9259 Shaughnessy Street, Vancouver, British Columbia, V6P 6R4
www.talonbooks.com

First revised edition, fourth printing: 2019

Typeset in New Baskerville and printed and bound in Canada
on 100% post-consumer recycled paper

Cover photo of Africville by Bob Brooks, courtesy of Nova Scotia Archives
and Records Management, Halifax
Cover design by Adam Swica

Talonbooks gratefully acknowledges the financial support of the Canada
Council for the Arts, the Government of Canada through the Canada Book
Fund, and the Province of British Columbia through the British Columbia
Arts Council and the Book Publishing Tax Credit.

Rights to produce *Consecrated Ground*, in whole or in part, in any medium by any group, amateur or professional, are retained by the author. Interested persons are requested to contact: Charles Northcote, Core Literary Inc., 140 Wolfrey Avenue, Toronto, Ontario M4K 1L3; tel.: (416) 466-4929; fax: (416) 707-2420; email: charlesnorthcote@rogers.com.

Consecrated Ground was first published in 1999 by Blizzard Publishing Inc.

Library and Archives Canada Cataloguing in Publication

Boyd, George Elroy, 1952–
    Consecrated ground / George Boyd. – Rev. 2nd ed.

A play.
ISBN 978-0-88922-666-1

    1. Blacks–Nova Scotia–Halifax–Drama. 2. Relocation (Housing)–Nova
Scotia–Halifax–Drama. 3. Africville (Halifax, N.S.)–Drama. 4. Halifax
(N.S.)–Drama. I. Title.

PS8553.O93574C65 2011   C812'.54   C2010-907124-7

For my brother,
the late Frank Stanley Boyd Jr.,
(December 23, 1943–October 3, 2010)

Consecrated Ground was first performed at the Sir James Dunn Theatre in Halifax, Nova Scotia, on Friday, January 14, 1999, under the auspices of Eastern Front Theatre, with the following cast:

CLARICE LYLE	Jackie Richardson
WILLEM LYLE	Jeremiah Sparks
SARAH LIED	Murleta Williams
JIMMY WILLIS	Lucky Campbell
GROOVEY PETERS	Anne-Marie Woods
TOM CLANCY	Chris Shore
REVEREND MINER	David Woods

Directed by Richard Donat
Set design by Stephen Osler
Lighting design by Leigh Ann Vardy
Stage Manager: Christine Oakey

Playwright's Note

Located in the north end of peninsular Halifax, Nova Scotia, Canada, the black enclave of Africville was composed of about forty families, and at any given time, up to six hundred people. The community was older than Canada itself, having been initially settled by the black refugees of the War of 1812. Through time, even more people settled, subsequently receiving land grants from many heads of state, including Queen Victoria.

Africville suffered, historically and prejudicially, from the government's blatant neglect, and by the 1960s Halifax City Hall considered it an eyesore and a shantytown. Rather than provide amenities to the community, the city relocated the city dump, an abattoir, and a prison adjacent to the village. Subsequently, they declared it unsanitary, bulldozed it, and relocated its people to public housing.

To this day, the tragedy is a very sensitive and contentious issue; in fact, relocation and compensation claims are still actively pursued in the courts.

Although many of the incidents contained herein did indeed happen (including the relocation of a family in a dump truck), *Consecrated Ground* is a fictionalized account of this catastrophe.

—*George Boyd, 1988*
Halifax, Nova Scotia

Ten Years Later

I hate to admit it, but it is indeed a truism: "time does fly." It's truly hard for me to grasp, almost implausible to me that this play was written and conceived more than ten years ago. Yet, time stands still for no one person, place, nor thing. Africville provides us no exception.

Since *Consecrated Ground* first appeared on stage in 1999 there have been a number significant developments appended to the Africville saga:

2002—Part of the former Africville site was declared a national historic site.

2005—A provincial MLA in the Nova Scotia legislature, called for a bill to issue a formal apology (but no compensation) to the surviving former residents.

2010—On 22 February, Halifax City Council ratified what it called the "Africville Apology." The Government of Canada established a 250,000-dollar fund, called the Africville Heritage Trust. Its aim is to design a museum and build a replica of the church. A cheque has since been delivered to the Trust. As of this writing, however, no sod has been turned.

Obviously, and in my very blunt opinion, what everyone seems to be missing is the fact that the destruction of Africville cannot possibly be compensated.

How do you compensate a people, a community, for its way of life? How do you compensate for the slow, painful, and very methodical dismantling of its soul; its essence?

Aren't we all still searching for those answers?

Perhaps, just perhaps, money might only be the temporary patch on the elbow when a whole new garment is in need.

—*George Boyd, December 2010*
Montreal, Quebec

SET AND SETTING

Consecrated Ground is set in the community of Africville in 1965. Our set is comprised of several hanging cut-outs in the background. These are individually lit, painted and formed to represent the various houses, Victorian and Georgian, that populated the site. These hang at different levels, providing a sense of depth. The light on the cut-outs switches to indicate the location of various scenes, i.e., for scenes inside the church, the church cut-out is appropriately lit. For outdoor scenes, all the cut-outs are lit.

The uppermost cut-out is of the church. At the end of the play, of course, this is the last piece to go black.

Stage right contains Willem and Clarice's house. Here we have a stove, a fridge, an old vinyl 1960s kitchen table, chairs, as well as a pull-down couch. All are cramped stage right, as these people live in one room. To the extreme right is a doorway with a curtain for a door which leads to what they refer to as the "back room."

Stage left is the interior of the church. A pulpit, of course, and about three pews. It's arranged diagonally for sight-line purposes, with the pulpit facing directly and squarely to the audience.

In "the pit" stands the well. A sign, authentic to Africville, reads: "PLEASE BOIL THIS WATER BEFORE DRINKING AND COOKING." During the intermission, the well is removed to make way for the final scene.

CHARACTERS

CLARICE LYLE: A lifelong resident of Africville and the wife of Willem. She's just had a baby, probably her last, as she's an older woman, older than her husband in fact.

WILLEM LYLE: Husband of Clarice; younger than her. He's from Annapolis Royal, Nova Scotia, and moved to Africville—into her home—when he married Clarice.

SARAH LIED: A matriarch of Africville.

JIMMY "DOUBLE-SPEAK" WILLIS: An Africville resident. He stutters and thus the nickname.

GROOVEY PETERS: The "loose" woman in Africville. Originally from Jamaica via Montreal.

TOM CLANCY: White and fresh out of social work school, he has been assigned to the Africville relocation project.

REVEREND MINER: The minister of the Seaview Baptist Church. This Africville church is one of the many he serves.

Act One

Scene One

The house lights dim to the a cappella sound of "Poem #1" from Joe Sealy's Africville Suite. The sound fades into AUNT SARAH humming a lullaby. She sits in a chair rocking Tully. It's mid to late dusk as CLARICE enters.

CLARICE:
Oh, he's gone now, Aunt Sarah, I better take 'em—

SARAH:
No-no, Clarice, I enjoys it! (*Beat.*) Why look, he be sleepin', Leasey. Sleepin' like a ... like a—

CLARICE:
Like a (*Beat.*) baby? ... Aunt Sarah?

SARAH:
Yeah! Like a baby!

CLARICE:
(*Chuckling.*) Aunt Sarah, the chile is a baby!

SARAH:
Well you know-what-I-mean! (*She chuckles. Beat.*) Where'd you say Willem bees? I hear he's the new choirmaster.

CLARICE:
Ain't that somethin'? That's where he is now, rehearsin'.

SARAH:
Oh ...

CLARICE:
Well they can rehearse all they want if you ask me.

SARAH:
I was always wonderin' how come you never join the choir.

CLARICE:
'Cause I can read me my music, Aunt Sarah, that's why.

SARAH:
What?

CLARICE:

Aunt Sarah I can read me my notes. Music notes. Sharps. Sharps and stuff. Sharps I tell ya. 'Cause every nigger know that choir put the flat in the pancake.

SARAH:

(*Laughing.*) Girl you better stop!

CLARICE:

And don'tcha be caught bakin' no bread when they sings. Why every woman in Africville tippy-toein' round here and askin', "Leasey? The choir rehearsin' today?" Now Aunt Sarah why they be askin' me that?

SARAH:

Why?

CLARICE:

'Cause they ...

CLARICE and SARAH:

(*In unison.*) *Flattt*!!

SARAH:

Now you better not tell Willem that! The choir sound fine to me.

CLARICE:

It is a fine choir, Aunt Sarah. Just I ... I love teasin' Willem about it that's all.

SARAH:

I think you wanna tell that man right about he's-self.

CLARICE:

Why? (*She chuckles.*) More fun like this, Aunt Sarah.

SARAH:

Oh the lovebirds!

CLARICE:

And Willem gonna be singin' a couple of solos soon he tells me.

SARAH:

Now see what I tell ya about coloured women? They push the men down, just to pull 'em up. Throw 'em in that corner to pull 'em into the other—no wonder our men be so confused!

CLARICE:

Aunt Sarah I don't do that!

SARAH:

You guilty as charged. Poor Willem prob'ly think you think he can't sing, the way you go on about that choir. Well he the best thing that ever happened to the Africville choir I tells us. They been soundin' real good since he come to Africville, and I'm gonna tell 'em some-such. Now git me some tea.

CLARICE:

Oh, all right. (*She goes about her business, then halts.*) Aunt Sarah why I always feel I'm your little girl. "Go git me some tea"— what I do? Git right up and run for your tea.

SARAH:

S'pose to give me my propers, Leasey. I'm old.

CLARICE:

Old?! Aunt Sarah you be older than the Hills-a-Rome! In fact, you been old ever since I met ya. I think your momma made history: first woman to give birth to a senior citizen! *Old*!!

They laugh.

SARAH:

Ain't tired though. Say? You sign them papers you was goin' on about?

CLARICE hesitates.

Leasey?

CLARICE:

(*Vacantly.*) Uh-hunh?

SARAH:

I say—those papers?

CLARICE:

I signed 'em. I'm puttin' everythin' in Willem's name. See, if anything ever happen to me, him and Tully be taken care of.

SARAH:

Little-girl, now I know what you doin', don't need to be repeatin' it. It just foolish-ins if you ask me. This land always been in your—

CLARICE:
Well this my family now, Aunt Sarah. I'm older than Willem. And If somethin' ever happen to me—I know Willem take care of himself—but I got a baby now. I got a son.

SARAH:
He'd take care a Tully. Ya know that.

CLARICE:
I know he would, that's why I trust 'em. I signed all the land—everythin'—over to 'em, and please don't start.

SARAH:
Now have I said a word? (*She chuckles.*)

CLARICE:
But Aunt Sarah I know what you're thinkin' and I know I'm doin' what's right. The lawyer downtown that I clean for say he do all the legal stuff *pro bono*. That means for free.

SARAH:
Little-girl? (*Beat.*) You a Smith, Willem be a Lyle.

CLARICE:
I'm a Lyle too, Aunt Sarah. So's Tully. This all for Tully.

SARAH:
Little-girl ...

CLARICE:
Aunt Sarah—you know when you mad at me you always call me "Little-girl." Why you mad at me now?

SARAH:
'Cause this is not necessarily!! (*She whispers.*) And Little-girl?

CLARICE:
Whaa?

SARAH:
(*Blurting.*) I don't care what lawyer wanna do a Sonny Bono!

CLARICE:
Pro bono!!

SARAH:
That too!

They laugh.

CLARICE:
Well it's done now. Everything in Willem's name. 'Ventually, Tully's.

SARAH:
Suit yourself.

CLARICE starts humming "The Storm Is Passing Over."

Why you hummin' that hymn?

CLARICE:
What hymn?

SARAH:
"The Storm Is Passing Over."

CLARICE:
Oh … I always hum that, it's my favourite.

CLARICE continues humming.

SARAH:
Well if the storm ain't come yet, how can it be passing over?!

CLARICE:
Aunt Sarah?! You sumpin' else. (*Beat.*) Maybe I put Tully in his basket now.

SARAH:
Just a little longer, 'kay? Leasey?

CLARICE:
Oh, all right … Lord, Sarah, you shoulda been his momma. You always holdin' 'em.

SARAH:
'Cause this child's been blessed. Look how late in life you had 'em. Tully be you and Willem's gift from God, I tells us.

CLARICE:
I know, but Momma had me late in life, maybe … I take after Momma.

SARAH:
Ain't no takin' after her a-tall! I mean ya met Willem so late in life. That's why ya had Tully so late. (*Pause.*) You and Willem all the times up here in this house wif the door closed. A "Do not disturb" sign on the door too, thank-you-very-much! I mean, whatcha all thinks?! You in the Ritz Carl-a-ton or sumpin?! This be Africville, girl! (*She laughs.*)

CLARICE:

Now Aunt Sarah don't be—

SARAH:

And don't be blushin' and goin' on over there, Leasey. Everyone knowed you weren't makin' no dinner with that sign on yer door!

They laugh.

CLARICE:

Oh, Aunt Sarah ...

SARAH:

But why y'all had to be so oblivious about it—

CLARICE chuckles.

What now?

CLARICE:

"Obvious," Aunt Sarah. Why we had to be so "obvious about it."

SARAH:

That too!

They laugh again.

CLARICE:

Aunt Sarah, like ... like don't you wish you would've had babies?

SARAH:

Girl I've had all you babies. I been all your mommas. I raised you when your momma was in-service. You was there.

CLARICE:

Yeah—I guess you was in-service too, right? To all of us.

SARAH:

Uh-hunh.

CLARICE:

And made me eat my carrots.

SARAH:

And your turnip greens.

CLARICE:

And to this day Aunt Sarah, I can't stomach me no turnip greens and no carrots!

SARAH:

That so?

CLARICE:

Uh-hunh. Willem say they sumpin' the mice nibble on!

SARAH:

(*Laughing.*) Good! 'Cause we ain't got no mice in Africville—we got *rats*!! Ever since that dump ...

CLARICE:

Yeah ...

SARAH:

Blame that one on me too, baby?

CLARICE:

'Course!

CLARICE:

And come to think of it Aunt Sarah—you was old back then.

SARAH:

Can't study it! (*Pause.*) I wonder what they rehearsin' for Sundee?

CLARICE:

Willem never said. Aunt Sarah you boilin' your water?

SARAH:

Hump! (*Offstage,* WILLEM, *solo, sings "My Lord What a Morning."*) That Willem now.

CLARICE:

Don't he sound precious, Aunt Sarah? Like a angel. Tully gonna have a voice just like him. You wait and see.

SARAH:

And look-it y'all a blushin' and bloomin' over there. 'Course he sound precious. I already tol' ya: the best thin' that ever happen to the Africville choir.

CLARICE:

Now what was we talkin' about? (*Beat.*) Oh-yeah, the government say "boil before drinkin'" so I boil.

SARAH:

Girl I been drinkin' out that well since I was Tully's size and ain't poisoned me yet. The gov'ment? The gov'ment also put that dump out there. Give us all rats. You truss the gov'ment?

CLARICE:

Aunt Sarah I got nothin' to say 'bout no governments. They mind their own business, I mind mine. And you were drinking that well water long before there was a dump. The dump old-ddd too! (*She laughs.*)

SARAH:

Can't study it!

GROOVEY enters carrying a pail.

GROOVEY:

(*Lifting the pail.*) Hi everybody!!

SARAH:

Groovey, the baby!

GROOVEY:

Lobster, Leasey, lobster! They're runnin' and the men be down there throwin' 'em ashore!

SARAH:

Humph! Lobster ol' poor people's food!

CLARICE:

Well it sound good to me. Aunt Sarah do you mind watchin' Tully a bit and I'll go get us some lobster!

SARAH:

Take all the time you want, Leasey. Groovey, you remember the "Do not disturb" sign?

GROOVEY:

Uh-hunh ... sure do!

CLARICE:

Aunt Sarah!

SARAH:

(*Laughing.*) And Leasey ... Leasey up here runnin' and tellin' everybody: "Willem be a carpenter. Willem be a carpenter. Willem be a carpenter." Well, Little-girl, we all knows Willem be a carpenter, but we also knows your cupboards is fixed!!

They burst out laughing.

GROOVEY:

Fixed?! Fixed 'er like a dog they did!!

CLARICE:

Fixed? Girl, I just had Tully ya know!

GROOVEY:

Well Groovey Peters ain't doin' that for nobody. Ya hear? Nobody. Sides, I got my, ah ... "special friend." And he don't want no babies!

SARAH:

Oh ... and who that be now, Groovey?

CLARICE:

Yeah, tell us.

GROOVEY:

Oh ... I ... dunno ... ah, one of yer, ah ... "higher-ups."

CLARICE:

Really?

SARAH:

Go-on.

GROOVEY:

Got me an account at Klines he did!

CLARICE:

You got an account at Klines?! Well baby they must be givin' 'em away is all I can tell ya. I mean ... who you give as you references?

They chuckle.

Then ag'in, with all them fellas comin' and goin' in yer place—(*She chuckles.*)—guess that ain't no problem is it?

SARAH:

No, but Groovey ... well where ya tell 'em ya work girl?

GROOVEY:

Whaa? ... Oh you two think I'm payin'?! Uh-unh. Groovey Peters got ... friends.

SARAH:

Rich friends I'm thinkin'.

GROOVEY:

Uh-hunh. Say? Who's dat white man down at de well with Jimmy? I mean, he kinda young for Groovey ... but ... Groovey, ah, gotta keep the books open like.

CLARICE:

I seen 'em too. Jimmy look real excited-like.

GROOVEY:

Groovey didn't get dat close, girl! Why, look at de way Groovey dressed!!

SARAH:

Yeah ... you is a sight all right.

GROOVEY:

(*Laughing.*) Aunt Sarah! (*Beat.*) Leasey? Do Groovey look dat bad?!

CLARICE:

Groovey-girl we're goin' catchin' lobsters ain't we? Ya want high-heels and lipstick or sumpin'?

SARAH:

Don't be temptin' that ol' fashion-plate, Leasey. She be down on the beach in gowns and tiaras and some-such.

CLARICE:

Well let's git. (*Beat.*) Aunt Sarah you sure you gonna be all right?

SARAH:

I'll be fine.

GROOVEY:

Bye, Aunt Sarah.

SARAH:

Bye.

CLARICE:

See ya in a bit.

As they exit they shuffle and sing-song, ad libbing.

CLARICE and GROOVEY:

(*In unison.*) Lobster! Lobster Aunt Sarah!! We gonna git lobster ... (*Etc.*)

They exit.

SCENE TWO

The next night, WILLEM approaches the well carrying a bucket. JIMMY sits there on the ground. He seems to have been under some stress and is preoccupied.

WILLEM:
Double-speak? That you over there? (*Beat.*) Whatcha doin'
sittin' out there in the dark?

JIMMY doesn't reply.

Double-speak?

JIMMY:
What?

WILLEM:
How can ya tell a man stutters by his sneeze?

JIMMY:
H-h-how?

WILLEM:
(*Chuckling.*) He goes ... "Ah-chew! (*Beat.*) Ah-chew!"

He laughs. JIMMY doesn't respond.

Now Double-speak we all know you eat so much lobster—you
stutter. You know?—Two-claws?! (*He laughs.*)

JIMMY:
S-s-shouldn't make no f-f-f-fun of a man's G-g-god-given
c-c-complaints.

WILLEM:
Hey, Double-speak, man—lighten up. The world ain't comin'
to an end.

JIMMY:
(*Softly.*) Is for me.

WILLEM:
What? Where's yer bucket?

JIMMY:
A-a-ain't got a b-b-bucket.

WILLEM:
Well whatcha doin' sittin' down here then? You fixin' to rob
somebody or somethin'?

JIMMY:
(*Excitedly jumping to his feet.*) No! No! No! No! ... I-I-I-I don't
s-s-steal, Willem!!

WILLEM:

I ain't sayin' ya do!! (*Beat.*) Just strange to be sittin' here by
yourself this late at night. *Man!!* You're one of the only
brothers in Africville that got a full-time job. You shouldn't be
mopin' around here unless you … (*Pause.*) Oh that it? You got
laid off?

JIMMY:

No-no, I-I-I still … da-da-da-drivin' my truck.

WILLEM:

Well then, you should be on top of the world. I mean you got
a job. And what else ya tell me? When ya joined the choir you
tol' me it was the first time a word came outta your mouth
without—

JIMMY:

S-s-stutterin' …

WILLEM:

Yeah, so why'd ya quit?

JIMMY:

C-c-cause I ain't g-g-gonna be here no m-m-more.

WILLEM:

You mean at the church?

JIMMY:

No-no-no-no-no … I-I-I mean h-h-here.

WILLEM:

Here?! (*He lowers his voice.*) You mean in Africville? You ain't
gonna be here in Africville no more?

JIMMY nods affirmatively.

Well where ya goin'?

JIMMY:

A-a-aways …

WILLEM:

I mean … where you *gonna* be?

There's a long pause.

JIMMY:

Y-y-ya gotta k-k-keep this a s-s-s-secret …

WILLEM:

Yeah …

JIMMY:

K-k-keep this a s-s-secret—you hear?!

WILLEM:

All right—it's a secret! It's a secret!

Pause.

JIMMY:

Ya g-g-gotta p-p-promise.

WILLEM:

I promise, I promise. (*Under his breath.*) Man-oh-man.

JIMMY sits down and stares off. WILLEM consults his watch.

JIMMY:

I-I-I sole my p-p-place.

WILLEM:

(*Incredulously.*) You whaa?! You sole yer—

JIMMY:

I-I-I dun t-t-tol' ya I—

WILLEM:

You sole yer place? (*He chuckles.*) That's a good one! Like somebody's gonna buy a place in Africville? Jimmy there's some miracles even Jesus can't make happen. (*He starts lifting his bucket.*) Unless you gonna be serious, I gotta get me goin'.

JIMMY:

I-I-I is s-s-serious, Willem. I-I-I ... is!

WILLEM:

Well who bought it?

JIMMY:

(*Blurting.*) The city!!

WILLEM halts abruptly.

WILLEM:

The city?

JIMMY:

Uh-hunh ...

WILLEM:

Halifax? ... City?

JIMMY:

Uh-hunh ... y-y-yeah.

WILLEM:

Man, how big a fool you think I am? You expect me to believe—

JIMMY:

It-it-it t-t-true. I-I-I got me, five thousand d-d-dollars.

WILLEM:

Five thousand *dollars*?! Now what's the city want with this ol' piece a land?

JIMMY:

T-t-they says w-w-we don't live w-w-well enough.

WILLEM:

Don't live well enough?! Well why don't they help us fix it up then?! (*Beat.*) Here I am livin' in the middle of Halifax in 1965—and I'm lugging water from a well?! *Don't live well enough*?! I mean if rats was money—man I'd be livin' me on some ol' tree-lined boulevard. And no dump would be my next-door neighbour either. And, and, the rats would have ta pay room and board! (*He chuckles.*)

JIMMY:

T-t-t-this my h-h-home, Willem. Born and raised here on t-t-t-this ground.

WILLEM:

Oh, you sound like Leasey.

JIMMY:

But ... but ... t-t-the white man s-s-say, we all g-g-gotta move.

WILLEM:

We all gotta move? (*He chuckles.*) He obviously ain't met Leasey yet. So where we all movin' to?

JIMMY:

P-p-place called U-u-uniacke S-s-square.

WILLEM:

That in Halifax?

JIMMY:

T-t-they call it t-t-the p-p-projects. On Gott-Gott-Gott—

WILLEM:

Gottingen Street. I seen the place. I never thought nothin' of it. I thought it was for city folk.

JIMMY:
It-it-it for us. They th-the projects, I-I-I tells ya.

WILLEM:
Well yer lucky if you ask me. You're gonna have what I ain't.
Now who ya say this white man was?

JIMMY:
Mister C-c-clancy. Ya-ya-ya gots ta k-k-keep this a secret, Willem
ya gots to keep this a—

WILLEM:
Yeah-yeah. (*Beat.*) Well I just hope this Clancy comes to see
Leasey and me. When ya gotta leave?

JIMMY:
Next week.

WILLEM:
Next week?! (*Pause.*) Man! If you need a hand movin' and all—

JIMMY:
I-I-I ain't g-g-gonna g-g-go.

WILLEM:
So you mean you really ain't sold nuthin'. You ain't signed
nuthin'?

JIMMY:
I signed ...

WILLEM:
Well the man own the property now, Double-speak. You gotta
move.

JIMMY:
C-c-c-can't force me o-o-o-out.

WILLEM:
If you signed the papers there's nuthin' you can do about it
now, Jimmy. It's too late.

JIMMY:
I-I-I ain't m-m-m-movin'.

WILLEM:
Suit yourself. (*He stands, lifting the buckets.*) Look, if you want
me to help you move or anythin' like that, I will. But now I
gotta get me goin'. See ya later.

WILLEM eyes him for a few moments.

You gonna stay here all night, Double-speak?

JIMMY:

Just a little b-bit.

WILLEM moves off. Lights dim on the well as he approaches the house.

SCENE THREE

WILLEM notices someone or something crawling. It is GROOVEY crawling towards the house. He drops his bucket and runs directly to her.

WILLEM:

Groovey! Ohmegawd ... Groovey!

She slumps into his arms.

GROOVEY:

(*Stirring; delirious.*) Please ... no mo' ... no ... don't hit me ... no mo' ...

WILLEM:

What happened?!

GROOVEY:

I ... I ... I was ...

WILLEM:

(*Calling.*) Leasey?! Leasey?! (*To GROOVEY.*) Here ... let's git to the porch.

He guides her to the porch where they sit down. GROOVEY stands and starts swinging wildly, attacking him.

It's me!! Willem! Calm down, now! Sit ...

GROOVEY does and openly weeps as CLARICE enters the porch.

CLARICE:

What is going on out—*Ohmygod,* Groovey?! Groovey what happened?! (*She glances at WILLEM.*) She's cut! Git some water! (*CLARICE starts wiping GROOVEY's face with the end of her apron.*) Boilin' on the stove! *Hurry!!* (*WILLEM hurries off.*) And some cloths!!

GROOVEY:

My ... shoppin' ... bags ...

CLARICE:

Shopping bags?!

GROOVEY:

Dey in de road.

CLARICE:

Willem will get the bags. What happened girl?! What happened to ya?

GROOVEY:

... walkin' ...

CLARICE:

Walkin?! Walkin' where?

GROOVEY:

... dey come ...

CLARICE:

Who come? ... (*Calling off.*) The water Willem!! Hurry up!!

CLARICE:

(*Aghast.*) My God, girl ... You're a mess.

> *GROOVEY resists.*

Just let me wipe your face now Groovey! Blood all over the place here ...

GROOVEY:

... dey slap .... dey hits Groovey ...

> *WILLEM enters with a basin and a cloth. CLARICE dabs and wipes GROOVEY's face.*

CLARICE:

What ya s'pose happened to her?

WILLEM:

Ya gotta ask, Leasey?

CLARICE:

Broom the coon, right?

GROOVEY:

(*Blurting.*) They broom and they kick and they spit—!

CLARICE:

Now take it easy child.

WILLEM:

Well that's what I thinkin', look at 'er. I mean we know what she do, *they* know what she do.

CLARICE:
Well I heard a broom the coon before, but usually ain't no women be involved.

WILLEM:
Oh yes! (*Beat.*) Maybe not in Africville, but they are.

CLARICE:
She say somethin' 'bout shopping bags in the road.

WILLEM:
I'll get them.

He exits.

CLARICE:
They hurt you, girl? You know? In that way?

GROOVEY:
... naw dey don'ts, girl ... dey just punch, and kick, and spit, and yell nigger whore, and ... and ... dey kicks some mores ...

CLARICE:
Where this happen?

GROOVEY:
On de road ... dis car come behind me ...

WILLEM:
(*Entering.*) Were you by yourself?

GROOVEY:
(*Blurting.*) Yes I be by me-self! (*CLARICE embraces her.*)

CLARICE:
You gonna be all right, honey ... all right ...

GROOVEY:
When de car swoosh by, sumpin' hit me in de head. I looks and den dey get come out de car, throwin' rocks, yelling, hittin' and kickin' ... I crawls ... Groovey crawls here ...

GROOVEY stands, yelling defiantly.

Dey don't know who Groovey Peters is!! Dey don't know ...

WILLEM:
Oh yes they does.

CLARICE:
Sit down now, rest. Rest ...

GROOVEY:

Wait till I tells de man!!

WILLEM:

What man?

CLARICE:

Some white big-wig, some man buyin' 'er gifts and 'spense accounts.

WILLEM:

So what?

CLARICE:

She thinks it real.

WILLEM:

(*In total disbelief.*) Jee-sus. Only thing real is one thing.

GROOVEY:

(*Yelling.*) My friend be different!! He gonna marry me!! And he gonna git dem dat do dis to Groovey!! He gonna git dem!!

CLARICE:

Shush, now—Willem you gittin' her all upset.

WILLEM:

Well somebody gotta talk that girl into some sense. (*Beat.*) Groovey—ya can't trust them. Any of them. They're good with words to yer face, but don'tcha turn yer back. They talk about this at work and laughs and grins, I hear 'em Leasey. And when they know you heard 'em, they all pleads none of them ever did it. Oh-no. Not them. Maybe not. But they laughs and slaps the ones on the back that do. And ... and ... see? Somehow that free 'em of the guilt. Ain't no fertile ground in their minds, just old fallow fields. And when it comes to niggers, that's just how they prefers it. Groovey?! You listenin' to me?!

CLARICE, hands rolling into fists, defiantly stands and looks WILLEM in the eye.

CLARICE:

Is now the time, Willem? This the 'propriate time?!

WILLEM:

When's the 'propriate time, Leasey?! When?! When she in a box?! She believe some white knight gonna ride into Africville and marry her?! Protect her?! He gonna laugh and say, "Stupid whor-r-r-e!!" Just like the ones that broomed her!! (*They regard one another for a few moments.*) I'm so tired of this!! (*Beat.*) 'Cause a what they do … we … suffer!!

He storms off and exits. CLARICE returns to GROOVEY.

CLARICE:
Come on, baby. Come on inside.

They exit into the house and shut the door.

SCENE FOUR

It is Monday morning. The abrupt and rude noise of bulldozers sounds as SARAH silently goes to the well. She carries two buckets and starts pumping water. Momentarily CLANCY approaches, carrying an attaché case.

CLANCY:
Howdy.

SARAH:
(*Reluctantly.*) Oh … hell-low.

CLANCY:
They sure start early in these parts, don't they?

SARAH:
You come for some water, Sonny?

CLANCY:
No-no, just passin' through, but I—

SARAH:
Oh.

CLANCY:
I was thinkin' how do they sleep with that bulldozer raging and going-on like that?

SARAH:
You know that dump just a recent fixture to Africville and I for one hates it. All that noise drive the rats into our houses.

CLANCY:
Shame.

SARAH:

Wasn't no dump here afore, just a recent fixture I tells us. They need a dump, so why not put it right next to where coloured peoples lives? That make sense to you, Sonny?

CLANCY:

Ah, I think, ah they—

SARAH:

Me neither! It got to be seen that the white man then don't think the coloured is human, right?

CLANCY:

I, ah, saw, ah, the—

SARAH:

That too! Don't gotta be no Philadelphia lawyer to figure that one out. 'Cause little ol' me with my grade-three schoolin'—I been readin'.

CLANCY:

Really?

SARAH:

Been readin' all about it. 'Bout South Africa.

CLANCY:

Oh, I thought you were referring to—

SARAH:

That too! I gits Jimmy's Sonny to go to the lie-berry for me. All kinds a books 'bout South Africa in the lie-berry. You read about South Africa, Sonny?

CLANCY:

No, I, ah ...

SARAH:

Didn't think so! See ya don't need learnin' to put this picture all together, Sonny. Age is all the learnin' I got, and this place be just like South Africa.

CLANCY:

But this is Canada, Mrs. ...?

SARAH:

Miss, Lied. But most around here call me Aunt Sarah.

CLANCY:

Aunt Sarah.

SARAH:

"Miss Lied" to you!

CLANCY:

Oh ... oh, I'm sorry, Aunt Miss Lied.

SARAH:

That's better.

CLANCY consults his attaché case as SARAH, slowly raising her spectacles, approaches and peers into his case.

My!! You sure got a lotta important papers in that-there bag.

CLANCY:

Yes, I, ah, guess I do.

SARAH:

And just 'cause it's Canada don't mean it ain't racist.

CLANCY:

Excuse me? Oh, ah, I'm by no means am sayin' that Aunt—

SARAH:

Now the Lawd never did bless you people with long memories, did he?

CLANCY:

Ex ... excuse me?

SARAH:

Miss Lied to you! (*Pause.*) Now, ya know what I figures?

CLANCY:

What, ah, Miss Aunt Lied?

SARAH:

I figures Africville be just another name for township—you heard of the townships in South Africa, ain't ya?

CLANCY:

Of course, the—

SARAH:

Well Africville be just like that! They put all the coloureds in one place, close to the white city so they got a ready stock of labour, like maids, butlers, and gardeners and cleaners and the like.

CLANCY:

I don't think I'd go that far ...

He finds the document he's looking for and closes his attaché case.

SARAH:

I would. 'Cept in Canada, we just use different words for township. We calls it a "community" or a "village" or some-such. To me, it just be a township. Plain and simple. No runnin' water like the townships. No plumbin' like the townships. Everything like the townships 'cept what it be called.

She continues filling the pail.

CLANCY:

Can I give you a hand with that?

SARAH:

My, you a polite Sonny, ain't ya? Well Sonny, I been fetchin' my water here for almost nigh eighty years. What's gonna stop me now?

CLANCY:

(*Pointing.*) That sign for one thing.

SARAH:

(*Contemptuously.*) It a gov'ment sign.

CLANCY:

Yes. It is.

SARAH:

Uh-hunh ...

CLANCY:

Well Aunt—Miss Lied (*Pause.*) You should—

SARAH:

See that dump, Sonny?

CLANCY:

Yes.

SARAH:

It a gov'ment dump. See that abattoir?

CLANCY:

Yeah ...

SARAH:

Gov'ment give 'em a licence. The gov'ment don't put no plumbin' in here. Why the gov'ment put all the coloureds here in the first place. No jobs 'cause the gov'ment. (*Beat.*) Now you think Sarah Lied truss the gov'ment? You think any coloured person in he's right senses truss the gov'ment and they signs?

CLANCY:

Well I never thought—

SARAH:

Didn't think so! And ya see, people don't usually be sleepin' here in the mornings, Sonny. You must a come up the road and seen everybody headin' out, didn't ya? (*Beat.*) Well where'd you think they was all goin'?

CLANCY:

It hadn't crossed my mind and—

SARAH:

To work! Most the womens be going to the south end to clean and scrub on their knees to make a few cents. The mens goin' almost all to pier nine. They waits in lines almost never to be picked for work. While the new white man who just showed up gets hired. So, "sleepin'?" Sonny? "Sleepin'?" We ain't got no time to be sleepin' in Africville. We too busy pickin' up the droppin's behind those white asses and too busy tryin' to put food in our chile's mouths.

CLANCY:

(*Consulting his file.*) You're Sarah Lied, right?

SARAH:

Now I done tol' you that! (*Beat.*) Hand me that pail.

CLANCY:

(*Handing her the pail.*) You use a lot of water for an—

SARAH:

Old woman? (*She chuckles.*) I always drops off a pail at Leasey's house. She got small Tully now to tend to in the mornin'.

CLANCY:

"Leasey?" Would that mean Clarice Lyle?

SARAH:

Why that her name proper. Yes.

CLANCY:

She's married to Willem?

SARAH:

My, all these big questions comin' outta such a little Sonny. But if ya must know, yes.

CLANCY:

I don't mean to pry, it's just that I have some business with him. (*Beat.*) Do you know if he's home?

SARAH:

He's at work! Down waitin' on the pier like the rest of 'em! Waitin' and waitin' and waitin'. Might git *one* day's work this month if he's lucky. Anyways I gots to be going.

SARAH starts off.

CLANCY:

(*Calling.*) Would you mind if I stopped by your place a little later, Mrs. Lied?

SARAH:

Miss! (*She halts.*) Now whatever for?!

CLANCY:

Maybe, ah ... some tea? Gets cold out here—you know? And I'd like to hear more of what you have to say about South Africa.

SARAH:

Well ... (*Pause.*) Guess everybody entitled to a little warmth— *and some schoolin'!*

CLANCY:

The yellow place?

SARAH:

(*Slowly.*) Why ... that's right. That's right. The yellow place on the knoll. Say what you doin' here in the first place Sonny?

CLANCY:

I'm here for the same reasons everybody else comes to Africville.

SARAH:

Oh? And just what might that be, Sonny?

CLANCY:

I'm a walker, Miss Lied. That's how I think. I enjoy the fresh air and the view from Africville's better than Point Pleasant

Park. The north end of the city is the best end of the city, I always say.

SARAH:

That so ...

CLANCY:

Yes it is.

SARAH:

Well don't let the secret out because we'll have all them white people 'scending on us with their poopin' dogs and stuff.

CLANCY:

(*Chuckling.*) Well I was just thinking, in fact. This place would make a good place for a park.

SARAH:

No it wouldn't!

CLANCY:

Why, ah, why not, Miss Lied?

SARAH:

Can't ya see? (*Beat.*) 'Cause people lives here, Sonny!! Ain't not a soul livin' in the Point Predential Park!

CLANCY:

(*Laughing.*) Caught me again, right?

SARAH:

Right! Well I best be gittin'. You tread careful 'round here now, Sonny. Right careful, you hear?

CLANCY:

Oh I will. Bye.

SARAH:

(*With slight contempt.*) And good day to ya.

> *She turns and exits. CLANCY kneels, opens his briefcase and rummages through his files.*

SCENE FIVE

Clarice and Willem's place. WILLEM peruses the newspaper. CLARICE is off in the back room.

CLARICE:

(*Off.*) Willem?

WILLEM:

Uh-hunh?

CLARICE:

Whatcha doin'?

WILLEM:

Hunh?

CLARICE:

I said, "Whatcha doin'?"

WILLEM:

Readin' the newspaper, baby.

CLARICE:

(*Off.*) Can you pass me Tully's blanket? It's on the table.

WILLEM obliges, handing it through the curtained doorway, then returns to his newspaper, preoccupied.

Thanks. (*Pause.*) The choir sounded real nice the other night.

WILLEM:

Yeah ...

CLARICE:

And you sounded like a angel when ya sang, "My Lord What a Mornin'." (*Beat.*) All by yourself too. A cappella.

CLARICE:

Hunh?

WILLEM:

Yeah ...

CLARICE:

'Course ya need more tenors if ya asks me. Always been a problem with the men folk in Africville: all scared to go sing the Lord's praises.

WILLEM:

I hear.

WILLEM flips pages. She enters carrying TULLY in his basket.

CLARICE:

My God though, Bethy Williams can sing! She like 'Retha Franklin. She hit them high notes—she straighten your hair.

She pauses, staring at TULLY.

I best be keepin' quiet before I wake this baby up, though that be impossible with Tully.

WILLEM:
Yeah ...

CLARICE:
You want some tea? A sandwich or somethin'?

There's no reply. CLARICE halts and regards him.

How about a nice, warm glass a poison?

WILLEM:
(*Preoccupied.*) Okay.

CLARICE:
Aunt Sarah got raped.

WILLEM:
(*Turning pages.*) Cool.

CLARICE:
Yep! By a Martian.

WILLEM:
I heard, yeah. Too bad hunh?

CLARICE:
Now she got an Albino baby with three heads.

WILLEM:
That so ...

CLARICE:
Willem, you ain't even listenin' to me!

WILLEM:
What?! Yeah! I'm listenin' ...

CLARICE:
And Aunt Sarah got a Albino baby with three heads, does she?

WILLEM:
Whaa?

She starts the kettle.

CLARICE:
Lately your mind been a million miles away, Willem. (*There's no reply.*) Willem?!

WILLEM:

(*Vexed.*) What, Leasey?! What is it? I'm tryin' to read the newspaper. Can't a man read a newspaper in this house?!

CLARICE:

You been readin' the newspaper a lot lately. Every day since last week. Why alla sudden this big interest in the news?

WILLEM:

Woman, I think you're struck.

CLARICE:

Well, ya never took such a notice of the newspaper before is all I'm sayin'.

WILLEM:

Well I guess I never had to.

CLARICE:

And ya got to now? What's that s'pose to mean?

WILLEM:

Milk and sugar in my tea, Lease.

CLARICE:

I know what ya take in your tea! I'm your wife!

WILLEM:

Are ya?! You got a husband? You got a real husband?

> *There's a pause.*

CLARICE:

(*Chuckling.*) Ya know, Aunt Sarah said to 'spect this.

WILLEM:

'Spect what?

CLARICE:

You know, husbands be sorta put out when their first chile arrives. The woman give the chile all the attention. (*Beat.*) I said, "And what about the wife? The man don't give her no attention a-tall." Now Willem, (*She giggles mischievously.*) you knows I luv-me my attention. (*WILLEM chuckles.*) I mean, how you think Tully got here? (*Beat.*) By he's-self?

> *They laugh.*

WILLEM:

Well baby, I know the postman been by quite a bit.

CLARICE:

Ain't no postman ever set foot in Clarice Lyle's house, so there!

WILLEM:

But I was just starin'. Babies don't come from no starin'.

CLARICE:

(*Tapping him playfully.*) Doin' more than starin'!

WILLEM laughs.

And where ya ever git that "Do not disturb" sign ta put on the door? Aunt Sarah ain't never let me live that one down yet. (*Mocking.*) "Oh-the-lovebirds, oh-the-lovebirds, oh-the-lovebirds!" You know how she does.

WILLEM:

Tell 'er I was just fixin' up a few things round the place.

CLARICE:

(*Standing; mockingly putting her hands on her hips.*) "Fixin' up a few things?!" And what I look like, a jigsaw drill?! 'Cause honey, you was workin' on me!!

They laugh loud and hard.

Sssshhh!! You'll wake Tully!

WILLEM:

Me? You laughin' just as hard. (*Pause.*) Look, your water's boilin'.

CLARICE:

Was in them days, baby! (*More softly.*) Was in them days.

She chuckles and goes to make tea. WILLEM returns to his newspaper.

Can't get your nose outta that paper, can ya?

WILLEM:

Just lookin', Leasey.

CLARICE:

For what?

WILLEM:

A job! A house!

CLARICE:

What do ya mean a house? We got a house right here.

WILLEM:

Tully's gonna git older.

CLARICE:

'Course, he just a baby.

WILLEM:

I mean, he gonna need his own room. Why we ain't even got a bedroom Leasey, just that ol' pull-down couch.

CLARICE:

And I been workin' on that.

WILLEM:

Oh, you have, have ya?

CLARICE:

Yep. All the *men* are gonna help ya build a add-on.

WILLEM:

That so?

CLARICE:

Yep, I been talkin' to all the *women*.

WILLEM:

Oh, you talked to the women—you ain't talked to the men.

CLARICE:

Willem ... and you a married man. It ain't the men that got the power. It's just we women let them *think* they got the power. A bedroom can be a mighty cold place when yer partner got a headache. Allll the time-ee!! (*She chuckles.*) You know what I'm sayin'?

WILLEM:

Well ... it just goes beyond a bedroom, Leasey. (*Earnestly.*) I mean, it goes beyond any room—living room, bathroom, playroom—it goes beyond rooms and add-ons.

CLARICE:

What?

WILLEM:

Well what about schools, Leasey?! What about a job? Honey we gotta face it—Africville is the problem.

CLARICE:

Oh it is, is it?

WILLEM:

Yes, it is. (*Pause.*)

CLARICE:

Now ain't that juss like some nigger from the Valley?

WILLEM:

Whaa?

CLARICE:

In fact, it just like some nigger from anyplace in Nova Scotia other than Africville.

WILLEM:

Leasey—

CLARICE:

Walkin' round with yer noses in the air—

WILLEM:

Leasey I never meant—

CLARICE:

—like, like there be a stench here. Oh, I knows we got the dump and the abattoir and the prison and the little white racists tauntin' us. But 'member Willem, the white man put all that here. Not us. It was pushed in our faces. It a white stench. The stench ain't black.

WILLEM:

Clarice all I'm sayin' is that I'm tired of hearin' how the white man did this and the white man did that. I'm tired of it, 'cause this black man wants to do somethin' too. I wanna work, I want my chile to go to a decent school and I wanna live in a decent house—not some scraggily ol' shack.

CLARICE:

Oh, so this all this is to ya, hunh? A "*scraggily ol' shack*"?!

WILLEM:

I'm not sayin'—

CLARICE:

My great-great-granddaddy built this outta his own hands, Willem. It was just him and the dirt, Willem. This land was given to us by Queen Victoria. Queen Victoria! And he farmed that ol' acid-ee, rocky dirt out there so he could feed his family.

He fished in the Bedford Basin. He did whatever was necessary, and he made and gave love out here, raisin' his children. And he was proud. So don't you dare—*ever!*—come and say to *me*—

WILLEM:

Clarice all I'm sayin' is that times change. I just want the best I kin provide for my family.

CLARICE:

This is the best, Willem!! This is the best!!

WILLEM:

What, Leasey? What's the best?!

He stands angrily, slamming his fist.

A drafty house?! Dirt roads?! No running water?! You can't even have a shower here!! What's the best, Leasey?! What?! This?!

He regains his composure and sits down.

I wanna job. I wanna home. I want the *hell outta Africville!!* (*Lowering his voice.*) And I'll have all those things, too. Just watch me.

CLARICE:

Over my dead body ... *over my dead body* Willem Lyle!! Tully's gonna be raised here—just like me!! Just like me!! Where he's loved ... *where's he's loved Willem!!*

WILLEM:

Leasey, all I meant was—

CLARICE:

No!! (*Pause.*) See, I better go for a walk now, 'cause if I don't? It'll be the first time I lay my hands on my husband without love behind it ...

Calmly, yet angrily, CLARICE walks out the door.

WILLEM:

Leasey?!

He slams his fist on the table.

Goddamnit!!

CLANCY sits alone in the church staring at the pulpit as REVEREND MINER comes brushing into the room, removing his overcoat.

REVEREND MINER:
Either you're early, or I'm late, boy.

CLANCY:
I'm early, sir. Tom Clancy.

REVEREND MINER:
Say ... we got some coloured Clancys here in Africville—any relation?

CLANCY:
No ... but, ah ...

REVEREND MINER:
Cool in here. Maybe I'll start the furnace.

CLANCY:
Can it wait, sir? I'm rushed for time.

REVEREND MINER:
You're rushed for time?

CLANCY:
Yes I have some people to see and—

REVEREND MINER:
So you're the one they "sacrificed." (*He chuckles.*) Lord, listen to me. I'm still thinking yesterday's sermon. I mean, you're the one they "picked."

CLANCY:
Yes. Is there something wrong?

REVEREND MINER:
No, no. It was just I was expecting someone a little older that's all. I thought you sounded young on the phone—but not this young. I mean, you're a kid. Just a boy, really. Relatively speaking.

CLANCY:
Relative to what?

REVEREND MINER:
Relative to what you're charged to do.

CLANCY:
I'm twenty-four, a graduate of Dalhousie University and the Nova Scotia School of Social Work. I have two degrees.

REVEREND MINER:
That's mighty impressive. When did you graduate?

CLANCY:
Last spring.

REVEREND MINER:
Oh ... master of the world!

CLANCY:
Sir, I—

REVEREND MINER:
Call me "Reverend" like everybody else.

CLANCY:
Life experience wasn't a prerequisite when the city posted this job. I simply applied. I got the job and you're the first one to mention—

REVEREND MINER:
I see. Well, "boy"—I'm sorry—"Mister Clancy." I—

CLANCY:
Call me what you want, Reverend. I've been called everything since I got on-site: "Sonny," "kid," "little boy," "man"— everything since I got on the site.

REVEREND MINER:
Boy—and don'tcha forget this—this job is gonna require a lot of life experience from you. A lot of soul searching and not a little grief. I mean, what are they doing down there thrusting a job like this on a kid?

CLANCY:
I guess you'll have to ask them. Anyway, as I mentioned, I'm really strapped for time, Reverend. Can we get down to business?

REVEREND MINER:
By all means.

CLANCY opens his attaché case.

CLANCY:

Here's your envelope sir, hand delivered. It's the agenda for the Mayor's Africville Committee meeting.

REVEREND MINER:

I see. Our friends at city hall are very efficient—aren't they?

He opens and peruses it.

CLANCY:

The committee will meet twice a month.

REVEREND MINER:

Yes, I already know.

CLANCY:

Sir?

REVEREND MINER:

I know you have an agenda and you probably have your speech ready. So let's not beat around the bush and get down to brass tacks. There's nothing you can tell me on behalf of the city that I haven't already discussed with the city. Nothing you can tell me that I already don't know about.

CLANCY:

Reverend?

REVEREND MINER:

It rather seems that the city was of the opinion that the performance of your duties left something to be desired. And at a little meeting they asked me to attend, they thought your presence wasn't particularly needed. It was agreed that I would help you bring your task to a swift and successful conclusion.

CLANCY:

(*Nervously.*) Yes, well … yes, ah, that was brought to my attention—the need for expediency and all—and well, as you apparently already know, unless we can get everyone to agree to our offer, the city is prepared to expropriate this land. That's not public knowledge yet, but we don't have much time. With your help, I believe we can convince everyone to sell and avoid expropriation.

There's a long pause.

Reverend?

REVEREND MINER:

Do you really know—do you really understand—what you're getting yourself into?

CLANCY loudly snaps the attaché case closed.

CLANCY:

It's not often a kid my age gets an opportunity like this, Reverend. I mean, I can write a book, maybe a master's thesis. Build a career based on what happens on this site.

REVEREND MINER:

Good, because Africville is more than anyone's "site." It's more than a headline or a paper for a master's thesis; a so-called "career-builder." It's a way of life. Now you keep asking me to keep quiet. Well I'm asking you about my concerns for the church.

CLANCY:

The church stays, Reverend. That's done, but without our agreement we'll have a circus on our hands.

REVEREND MINER:

No "*we*" won't. You boy, you and the city will have a circus on your hands. I mean what's the problem here—the *real* problem here? (*Beat.*) They say they can't provide water and basic amenities to the people here? Well in the years to come—and you mark my words—when they build a park or a shipping terminal or whatever they decide to build here—just see if *those* establishments don't have paved roads, sewage and running water, okay? Just observe … observe … and mark my words.

CLANCY:

Are you saying the city's lying, Reverend Miner?

REVEREND MINER:

I'm saying they're not telling *all* the truth. I'll tell the whole truth … at the appropriate time.

CLANCY:

All I want, Reverend, is a full and fair hearing, that's all. I mean before the onslaught of opinions and editorials and—

REVEREND MINER:

Just because I listen to the city's plans, doesn't mean I condone them. I realize the inevitable—

CLANCY:

All I'm asking for is a chance. I can make this a smooth transition.

REVEREND MINER:

For who? A smooth transition for who? You and the city?

A long pause.

All I need to know is does the church stay?

CLANCY:

It does. That's correct.

REVEREND MINER:

Then good-day to you sir. I've got to get some warmth in God's house.

REVEREND MINER exits.

SCENE SEVEN

All save the REVEREND and CLANCY have gathered at the church.

JIMMY:

W-W-What you think the-the-the—

GROOVEY:

"The Reverend wants?!" Spit it out, fool, 'cause Groovey Peters got her no patience today.

SARAH:

(*Admonishing.*) Groovey! Now what I tell you?

CLARICE:

Whatcha think, Aunt Sarah?

SARAH:

Well, the last time Sarah been at a "family meeting"—

WILLEM:

I ain't from Africville. What do that mean, Leasey? "Family meetin'"?

JIMMY:

It-it-it—

SARAH:

Yes we is. We all family, son, and we all in God's church.

CLARICE:

It means all of us folk here gets together, honey. And just *us*
folks. We ah … (*She chuckles.*) manage to avoid invitin' the
whites.

SARAH·

And it mean somethin' import be up. We don't call a family
meetin' to talk foolishin's. (*Beat.*) Hear that Groovey?

GROOVEY:

Now Groovey Peters be sittin' right here, Aunt Sarah.

The REVEREND enters, removing his coat, and goes to the pulpit.

REVEREND MINER:

Now I'm not gonna preach to y'all—(*He gets down and stands
on the floor, looking at them.*)—I'm not going to pontificate, I'm
gonna elucidate …

GROOVEY:

Hell-oh!

SARAH:

Groovey! Now what I tell ya?!

CLARICE:

Go ahead, Reverend.

REVEREND MINER:

Now I know ya all seen that white man around here a lot.

JIMMY:

Oh Lawd.

REVEREND MINER:

We all seen him, we know that. Well he's not here 'cause he
likes the view—

JIMMY:

He's here on ba-ba-ba-ba-ba-ba-ba-ba—

GROOVEY:

Now the damned fool sound like a sheep!

SARAH:

Groovey!

JIMMY:

—business!

SARAH:

What kind of business, Reverend?

REVEREND MINER:

City business. He's here because he's been instructed by his bosses—the city—to buy your land.

CLARICE·

Well we ain't sellin'!

WILLEM:

Leasey will you *listen* to Reverend Miner?

CLARICE, holding TULLY, stands and gathers her purse.

CLARICE:

No, let's go home, Willem. 'Cause we ain't sellin' so this ain't none of our business.

REVEREND MINER:

I think you should stay, Leasey. Really.

WILLEM:

I wanna hear what the Reverend's gotta say. If it affects Africville—I wanna hear.

Reluctantly she sits.

REVEREND MINER:

Like I was saying, this man—this Clancy—he's here on official city business. Now they're going to develop this land and they're making financial offers. Offering those with families a place in Uniacke Square.

JIMMY:

The-the-the projects!

CLARICE:

Then they gotta pay us.

REVEREND MINER:

Yes. A fair price—the city assures me. Now think of this: you all be close by. You'll have all the amenities the white folks have—water and plumbing. You'll be closer to grocery stores, hospitals, and schools. And—we'll have the church right here in Africville.

SARAH:

Hallelujah!

CLARICE:

(*Standing.*) Now when the city gonna be fair to niggers? Never have, never will be, I say. (*To WILLEM.*) I tol' ya this ain't got nothing to do with us, Willem. We ain't sellin'. Now c'mon.

CLARICE exits with TULLY. WILLEM stays.

GROOVEY:

Rev'rund Miner?

REVEREND MINER:

Yes, Groovey?

GROOVEY:

You been talkin' to de city?

REVEREND MINER:

I have.

GROOVEY:

And you never told us?

REVEREND MINER:

The meetings were confidential. And I was forced to keep my mouth shut or I probably would not have been invited. We wouldn't even possess this much information. Now keeping the church was a struggle—but that's the great thing. We all know what the church means to coloured folk: it's our monument to those who died on the middle passage—every spirit that lies on the bottom of the Atlantic.

ALL:

(*Variously.*) Amen ... That's right ... Uh-huh ... (*Etc.*)

REVEREND MINER:

The church embodies all that we do: it's where we baptize our young, and not-so-young. Where we get hope, when hope doesn't appear to be on the horizon. Where we mourn and get strength for the loss of a loved one. The church, as you all know, is a living monument. A testament to a race of black people; a proud, hard-working, and loving people. Our divine power and spirituality—all of our mothers. It is the very cement which our community was founded upon. Our sustenance when we're weak—

SARAH:

Yes, Lord.

REVEREND MINER:
Our warmth when we are cold. Our very essence itself.

SARAH:
Praise God.

REVEREND MINER:
So just because we live down the street—a little way from here—Africville will never die. In this church, our soul shall live.

GROOVEY:
You said you wasn't gonna preach!!

SARAH:
(*Standing up.*) That was a *great* sermon and such, Reverend. Fancy words and all. But lemme tell you this: it's well known that if you lay down with dogs, you come up with fleas.
    She sits.

ALL:
(*Variously.*) Go on Aunt Sarah! I hear ya! (*Etc.*)

REVEREND MINER:
Africville will not be lost—you'll all be neighbours in the city.

JIMMY:
G-g-g-good! Then we can all m-m-m-move together!

REVEREND MINER:
Where there will be no bulldozers. No dumps. No abattoir stench and above all—no rats.

JIMMY:
They-they-they gittin' bigger than the c-c-c-cats, Reverend.

GROOVEY:
So what do we do now, mun?

REVEREND MINER:
Go home—
    All save REVEREND MINER start to exit.
Wait for this white man, this Mister Clancy, to approach you with an offer. If you decide to move, he assures me everything will be handled in an orderly fashion.

GROOVEY:
Good! (*Standing.*) What he look like, honey?

SARAH:

Groovey, git your mind out the—(*She grabs her arm.*)—c'mon, girl.

All exit, the REVEREND stands alone.

Blackout.

SCENE EIGHT

Clarice and Willem's place. CLARICE is off in the back room; we hear something thumping the floor.

CLARICE:

Damn rats!!

As CLARICE enters, we hear the bulldozers start.

Oh Lord, please have mercy on me!!

She goes to the crib and looks in on TULLY.

My son, I don't know how you can sleep through all of this? I just dunno ...

SARAH enters.

SARAH:

Leasey!—the rats! My kitty's scamperin' this mornin'.

CLARICE:

You ain't kiddin'!

SARAH:

It's that racket from the bulldozer I tells us.

CLARICE:

All that bulldozer is doing is pushing trash from one side ta the other. And every time they do it, I gotta deal with these damn rats.

A rat hurries across the floor.

SARAH:

(*Startled; pointing.*) Oh!!

CLARICE:

Looked it scamper!! Looked it!!

CLARICE grabs a broom, smashing and stabbing the floor as she runs haphazardly around the place, lifting or pushing whatever is in her path. SARAH surveys the madness.

SARAH:

Why you like you playin' hockey, girl! (*She laughs.*)

CLARICE:

Git out my way, git out my way! (*Stabbing.*) Damn! Git outta my way!

SARAH laughs initially, but screams in horror, eyes blanching, as she spies a rat nearing her.

SARAH:

Oh me Lawd Jesus!

She hops on top of a chair, lifting her skirts and running on the spot.

Git it Leasey, git it!! Git it 'fore it—

CLARICE:

Don't be screaming-jumpin' round me! White womens screams and jumps! We niggers fights!!

SARAH:

Git it git it git it!! (*She laughs.*)

CLARICE stops suddenly, breathlessly slumping into a chair.

CLARICE:

I's ... I'm, I'm too tired to git it!

SARAH:

Uh-hunh ... (*She laughs.*) Leasey, how I git up this chair, girl? (*Laughs.*) Help me down.

CLARICE, laughing, obliges as TULLY suddenly erupts, crying. SARAH goes to the crib. The bulldozers stop.

CLARICE:

(*To the ceiling.*) Thank ... you ... Jesus!!

SARAH:

Aw, Tully don't like rats, either.(*She picks him up.*) You the best gift ever.

WILLEM enters.

WILLEM:

Hi Leasey.

CLARICE:

Hi baby. No work?

SARAH:

Again?

CLARICE surreptitiously signals for SARAH to "shush."

WILLEM:

(*Angrily.*) What the hell can I do about it?! The man don't hire us—he hires the new white guys!

CLARICE:

We was just sayin' is all, Willem. No need to be nasty.

WILLEM:

But you-all act like I don't wanna work or somethin'. (*Beat.*) Why you all outta breath, Leasey? And where's the paper? Jesus. (*Gestures to TULLY.*) And what's he yellin' about?

CLARICE:

Only you and a Walter Cronkite ask so many questions, Willem.

SARAH:

Leasey ... (*She chuckles.*) Leasey was chasing rats.

WILLEM:

Oh ...

SARAH:

Like a bull in a china shop, she was!

She laughs. WILLEM goes to SARAH and takes TULLY.

WILLEM:

(*To the baby.*) How's my big boy, hunh? Yeah, it's all right now, Daddy's here ... Daddy's here now.

CLARICE:

(*Sharply.*) He was all right before his daddy got here, thank-you-very-much.

WILLEM:

Leasey, please. Don't start. The paper ain't here yet?

CLARICE:

Aunt Sarah hand that man the paper, please, before I have to get up and knock him out.

SARAH obliges and WILLEM takes the paper and TULLY into the back room.

SARAH:

Leasey? Weren't I fetchin' water and guess who was down by the well?

CLARICE:

Who?

SARAH:

That white man—a boy really.

CLARICE:

A white man? Another one?

SARAH:

Uh-hunh ...

Pause.

CLARICE:

Welll?!

SARAH:

Well whaa?

CLARICE:

Did you ask this white man what he was doin' here, Aunt Sarah?

SARAH:

Now I just tol' ya what I saw. I think he the one the Rev'rend was talkin' 'bout. But, Leasey, if I ask every white man that come to Africville what he was doin' here, Groovey be after me for edgin' her business.

CLARICE:

And we all knows you does pose a threat to Groovey, Aunt Sarah! (*She chuckles.*)

SARAH:

Humph! (*Pause.*) Still plenty a mileage on this ol' Cadillac!

CLARICE:

(*Laughing.*) Aunt Sarah you better stop!

SARAH:

No no. You always teasin' me bout my age, Leasey—well look-it you. You're whatcha call, "older." Well, your sun ain't quite set girl, but it's headin' for the Rockies!

CLARICE:

Aunt Sarah! (*She laughs.*)

SARAH:

> And before I forget, you can tell that man of yours that if his actions ain't the be-all-and-end-all I don't know what is! He never say how-ya-do or kiss-yer-ass to me. He just grunt and grab Tully.

CLARICE:

> (*Whispering.*) Aunt Sarah, I hope, I pray, work comes soon. He so ornery I tells ya. He bangin' this pot and slammin' that door and then he be so quiet-like. He just read the papers.

SARAH:

> Umph-umph-umph—*men!* They so confused. Oh well. I best be goin' I tells us.

CLARICE:

> Here. I'll walk ya to the door. Bye, Aunt Sarah. See ya later. (*Returning.*) Willem? I might be goin' into Halifax some-time this week. I need material.

WILLEM:

> Suit yourself.

> *A great noise and hullabaloo comes from outside.*

GROOVEY:

> (*Off, crying.*) Leasey?! ... Leasey?!

CLARICE:

> What ... the ... hell ...

> *GROOVEY, noisily, and out of breath, bursts into the room. She is hysterical and crying. TULLY cries again.*

GROOVEY:

> Groovey dun know what dey doin'! I dun know!

CLARICE:

> What is it?! What is it?!

WILLEM:

> (*Entering with a crying TULLY.*) Jesus Groovey we got a baby ya know!

GROOVEY:

> They gone, Leasey! Gone!

CLARICE:

> Who? Whatcha talkin' about?!

WILLEM:

This racket better calm down!

GROOVEY:

Go and look, Leasey! Go and look!

CLARICE:

Go and look at what, baby?! What—

GROOVEY slumps her head into her hands and cries.

GROOVEY:

Jimmy! Da Willises move out ... Dey move out ...

CLARICE:

People move in and outta Africville every day, Groovey.

GROOVEY:

(*Sobbing.*) But not like dis ... not like dis ...

CLARICE:

Hunh?

GROOVEY:

In a garbage truck?! Dey move 'em in a garbage truck!!

CLARICE:

Now, Groovey, ain't nobody moving in garbage trucks. What's wrong with you, girl?

GROOVEY:

There's nothing wrong with me I know what I saw! I know what I saw!! Dem ... white ... bastards!! Dem mens—wif dere overalls and gloves on, like dey was gonna be contaminated—*contaminated*!! Dey just threw Bonita's and Jimmy's furniture on day truck. Dey broke stuff ... Dey joked among themsell ... it was ... was ... and poor Bonita. She cry and beat on Jimmy's chest ... Now da dozers be dere ... *dey knockin' it down*!!

CLARICE looks about, hands quivering, eyes wondering, then she and GROOVEY bolt out the door, as WILLEM exits to the back room with TULLY.

Scene Nine

WILLEM enters the room, sips his beer, and peruses a newspaper that's sprawled on the floor. A knock comes from the door. He looks to it, then goes and opens the door.

WILLEM:

Yes?

CLANCY:

Mister Lyle? (*Pause.*) Hi, my name's Clancy. (*He extends his hand.*) Tom—

WILLEM:

I know who you is.

CLANCY:

Yes, ah … Tom Clancy. (*He drops his hand.*) I was wondering if I might speak with you for a few seconds.

WILLEM:

Okay.

Both awkwardly stand there for a few seconds.

CLANCY:

(*Clearing his throat.*) Might I come in?

Pause.

WILLEM:

Okay.

CLANCY enters, looking about.

CLANCY:

Your wife's not home I take it.

WILLEM:

That's right. (*They stand awkwardly.*) Have a seat. (*Beat.*) Like a beer?

CLANCY:

No thanks. (*He sits.*) Mind if I smoke?

WILLEM:

No.

He lights up, leaving his Zippo on the table, and coughs violently.

CLANCY:

I ... just started ... to ... to ... smo ... smoke!

WILLEM:

(*Chuckling.*) Oh ...

CLANCY:

Now ... (*He coughs.*) as I was saying, I represent the City of Halifax, I'm a social worker—here's my card—and I've been asked to speak to the families here and—

WILLEM:

I know, I know.

CLANCY:

Uh-hunh yes. Well you're not from here are you, Mister Lyle? "Willem," if I may.

WILLEM:

No.

CLANCY:

Where are you from?

WILLEM:

Annapolis Royal. I'm a carpenter. Visited here and met Leasey and got married. Look Mister Clancy—

CLANCY:

Tom. Call me Tom.

WILLEM:

Tom. You're wasting your time. My wife ain't givin' this place up. If it were up to me—I would've been outta here yesterday—but you know women.

CLANCY:

(*Smiling.*) That I do. But (*Beat.*) why would you leave?

WILLEM:

I may be coloured, Mister, ah, Tom, but I don't like slums. White people believe coloureds like slums. Well we don't.

CLANCY:

I'm certainly not saying that, Willem.

WILLEM:

I'm sure you ain't. Not in this house anyway. See? I was brought up in the country—on a farm. Good, solid houses; proud people. We all worked and produced. *We* never had no outside jobs, we made our own jobs. Here—if the white man don't wantcha—you outta luck. And we're down on our luck in Africville I tell ya.

CLANCY:

I understand. So what are you going to do?

WILLEM:

(*Shrugging his shoulders.*) Don't rightly know, but I tell ya, things gotta change. I got me a little mouth to feed now.

CLANCY:

Yes, I noticed the crib. Boy or a girl?

WILLEM:

Boy.

CLANCY:

Congratulations.

WILLEM:

Thanks. (*Pause.*) Mister Clancy—

CLANCY:

"Tom," okay? Call me "Tom." Might I have a coffee?

WILLEM:

Just put a pot on. Milk? Sugar?

CLANCY:

Both, thanks. Now you said you wanted to leave, right?

WILLEM:

Damn right. Somethin' gotta happen round here.

CLANCY:

Well what would you say *if*—if I said I could help you out?

> *WILLEM shrugs. CLANCY opens his attaché case and withdraws a file.*

You now possess the deed to this place, Willem. Mrs. Lyle— according to this, Mrs. Lyle has just—

WILLEM:

Clarice.

CLANCY:

Yes, Clarice. She just signed it over to you—just recently in fact. (*Pause.*) Look, Willem, I guess the best way to talk about this is to be frank. I'm sure you're aware of Africville's reputation. I mean people call it the "slum by the dump" among other things right?

WILLEM nods affirmatively.

Well the city wants to rectify this problem, correct it if you will. You see we realize there's no running water here, no plumbing, and well—you know—the dump's next door. The abattoir and, well, I could go on. Despite all of this—you live here. Now it's no longer acceptable to the City of Halifax that Negroes live in one place, Willem, and white people another. You follow me?

WILLEM:
Uh-hunh.

CLANCY:
You know, a place where the kids don't get a proper education—I guess what I'm trying to say (*Beat.*) is all the benefits that white citizens get and take for granted. So, I'm rather happy to inform you that the city has decided to deal with the site.

WILLEM:
"The site"?

CLANCY:
Yes. You know … Africville. We want to buy all the families out. Everything. Every door, board, lamp post and window. Everything.

WILLEM:
Everything?

CLANCY:
Everything.

WILLEM:
Just like that?

CLANCY:
Just like that.

WILLEM:
Even the church?

CLANCY:
No, not the church. The city's not in the habit of desecratin' sanctified ground—but everything else you see here. Everything. The city wants to buy it fair and square.

WILLEM:

I see.

CLANCY:

Now we're offering fair price for the properties. We're even giving five hundred dollars to those people who don't possess a deed as a sign of good faith. Now lemme see ... (*He consults his file.*) You possess the deed. The deed's in your name.

WILLEM:

This land been in Leasey's family for years—well over a century.

CLANCY:

Well, we'd be prepared to offer you five thousand dollars. In fact I have the cheque right here, Willem.

He produces an envelope containing a cheque and a large envelope and places them on the table.

You look suspicious.

WILLEM:

You wanna give us five thousand dollars (*Looking about.*) for this?

CLANCY:

Yes. See Willem, the city realizes it's been, well let me put it this way, less than an ideal administration to the people of Africville. We want you people—all our people in fact—to live and walk and drive on paved roads. We want all our people to have street lights. We want you to live in a place where the police and the ambulances aren't afraid to come and are nearby. We want you to live close to services, like grocery and drug stores, and we want your kids to have proper schools. I mean, you've got a young one to think about now, Willem.

WILLEM:

But where would we go?

CLANCY:

Well, we're building a new housing development in town. You know, on Gottingen Street?

WILLEM:

Yeah, walked by it once or twice.

CLANCY:

See? The houses there have running water and plumbing. Furnaces. No more gathering wood or dealing with coal—

these work off oil. The schools are down the street and there's a grocery store just a block away. And we're prepared, the city that is, to give you the first year's rent free. Of course, you're free to seek your own residence, but a place in Uniacke Square is reserved for you and your family.

WILLEM:

Uniacke Square ... yeah, Double-speak was talkin' about that place.

CLANCY.

Ah, "Double-speak"?

WILLEM:

Just a friend.

CLANCY:

Oh. Anyway, what I have here is a simple contract. All you have to do is sign it and all that I just described is yours. I mean, your family's and yours.

WILLEM makes coffee. CLANCY walks to the window.

My God it's beautiful out here though isn't it, Willem? Especially at night. I always say it's like you're in the middle of the universe. I mean with all the city lights twinkling around you, it looks like you're surrounded by stars. (*Beat; he chuckles.*) Sorry, I wax poetic.

WILLEM:

No, everybody says that.

CLANCY:

Well it's true.

WILLEM:

You talk to many other people out here Mister Clancy? I mean, besides Double-speak?

CLANCY:

Who's this "Double-speak," Willem?

WILLEM:

Jimmy Willis. (*Suddenly angry.*) And ain't no garbage trucks moving us!!

CLANCY's face goes limp.

CLANCY:

Now that was very unfortunate, but all the moving trucks were booked. And you don't know how the city works downtown. There's clerks that've never been to Africville and they probably thought they were moving some office furniture from a city warehouse and they sent that garbage truck. I know it wasn't intentional and I've been assured by the city this will not happen again. I was very distressed. So what's it to be, Willem? I mean, you've made no secret that you're not happy here. Don't you want a good school for your son?

WILLEM:

Who—Tully? Yes.

CLANCY:

Good (*Pause.*) I, ah, just think you should have a lawyer look over this document. Take it to a lawyer, okay? (*He's packing up.*) Because it's gotten back to the city some moving issues have been noted, and we want people to be assured that this is all above table. So now the city wants me to tell everybody to take the documents to a lawyer. I leave it with you.

WILLEM:

I gotta talk with Leasey.

CLANCY:

(*Taking back the envelope.*) Yes, of course, speak with your wife. I'm sure she'll agree it's the right thing to do. It's the only thing to do. I'll be out of your hair then.

He stands and extends his hand. WILLEM shakes it.

WILLEM:

You're forgettin' your lighter.

CLANCY:

No no, you keep it. There's plenty where that came from. It's a Zippo. Has the city's coat of arms on it.

WILLEM:

Well I … I don't smoke.

CLANCY:

Maybe someone you know does. Listen, Willem, I'll drop by again. If you have any questions you've got my card. See you later.

CLANCY exits, as WILLEM sits at the table. Fondling the lighter, he glances over the contract.

SCENE TEN

Pandemonium in the Lyle household. CLARICE enters preparing a thermos and filling a sandwich bag. WILLEM is hurriedly grabbing his tools, coat, gloves, etc.

WILLEM:

Hurry, baby, hurry. I was s'pose to be there a minute ago.

CLARICE:

I'm rushin'. Ohmygod, Willem, work? I mean, real work?!

WILLEM:

For a few days straight anyways. White men don't wanna work over the holidays, so they—

CLARICE:

—*call* us. When you gonna be home?

WILLEM:

Aunt Sarah took the call. The man say long shifts, so I don't know. You ready?

CLARICE:

Almost.

WILLEM:

Oh … I forgot to get water from the well.

CLARICE:

I kin manage. Willem calm down, honey you're so excited.

WILLEM:

Okay … I'll try.

CLARICE:

(*Handing him a sandwich bag.*) Here ya go. Didn't put no turnip greens in there, either.

WILLEM:

(*Laughing.*) What would I do without ya, Lease?

CLARICE:

Baby you'd starve, 'cause ya can't even boil water without burnin' it!

They laugh again. She goes and picks up TULLY.

WILLEM:

Now listen to me Leasey. Look like a storm comin', but there's plenty a wood out there. If ya need anythin' call me on Aunt Sarah's phone. Okay?

CLARICE:

Okay.

WILLEM:

But don't call me unless it's important, 'cause it's hard to reach me down the pier.

CLARICE:

Okay, baby.

He kisses her quickly. He starts off, but returns and kisses his son.

WILLEM:

See ya, baby-boy.

As he exits, CLARICE follows him to the door.

CLARICE:

(*Calling.*) We luv you too, Willem. Bye!

SCENE ELEVEN

CLANCY is in the church sitting in a pew with his attaché case open beside him. He's distracted and preoccupied. He walks behind the pew and opens the big Bible, perusing with his finger. He looks closer and absently whispers.

CLANCY:

My God ... there's deaths and births and weddings in here dating from the eighteen-hundreds!

After flipping a few more pages he steps down and sits in a pew, lights a cigarette, and of course, coughs. We hear a door slam behind him, yet we see nobody. CLANCY, stubbing his cigarette, stares straight ahead.

That you, Reverend?

There is no reply.

You know, Reverend, here I am sittin' in a church in Africville. I mean, my friends would call it a "nigger" church. Here I am

67

sittin' in this "nigger" church in Africville. I should be at the Boat Club, sipping whiskey with my buddies and laughing about the dirty niggers in Africville. But ya know, Reverend? (*Swigs.*) I don't feel like laughing. I don't feel that way ... I mean, most of the places I been to out here, you can eat off their floors they're so waxed and polished ... Look, I believed ... I believe what I was told. I think what I'm doing is right. I'm doing the right thing.

JIMMY:

(*Entering.*) M-m-m-mister Clancy?

CLANCY is startled and turns towards the voice.

CLANCY:

Jimmy?! ... What the hell are you doing here? I thought you were Reverend Miner ...

JIMMY:

Ma-ma-ma-mister Clancy? ... I need a c-c-c-c-come back to Af-af-af—

CLANCY:

Africville.

JIMMY:

I still have the money you gave me. Most of it. I can buy back my land, rebuild my house.

CLANCY:

That's impossible!

JIMMY:

But my kids ... they-they-they run the streets, wild ... and ... and-and-and ... we have no ... we-we-we—

CLANCY:

You signed, you got—

JIMMY:

I-I-I ... but ... I-I-I ... don't know my fa-fa-fa-family no mores. Kids don't listen to me. They runs the streets, all hours of the nights. I-I-I-I can't com-com-com-plain to the neighbours, cause I-I-I-I don't knows who they bees. Please, Mister Ca-Ca-Ca-Clancy, I needs to—

Glaring at JIMMY, CLANCY slams the attaché case shut and walks past him.

CLANCY:

I'm sorry, but you signed. There's nothing I can do!

JIMMY:

But Mister Clancy?!

CLANCY exits.

SCENE TWELVE

There comes a humongous sound: a storm at the well. CLARICE enters, dressed only in a billowing housecoat and slippers. She gets to her knees, trying to clear the pump spout of ice. Very low, we hear TULLY crying; and in the far background, the choir rehearsing a hymn.

CLARICE:

Momma's comin', Tully. Momma's comin'. I just need some water ...

She gets to her feet again and pumps. Water drools slightly. She bends again, trying to clear the spout. Still quite low, we hear TULLY crying. CLARICE now cocks an ear towards the sound.

(*Muttering.*) Tully ... that you, baby? Momma be right there ... just gittin' water for your formula ...

TULLY's wailing intensifies, then abruptly stops as does CLARICE. She cocks an ear to the wind.

Tully?

She gets to her feet, looking in the direction of the house.

(*Louder; concerned.*) Tully?

She runs towards the house.

Tully?! ... Baby?!

She enters the house, dropping her pail on the table and enters the back room. We hear screeches and shrieks. Finally she emerges. And as the stage darkens she's lit in a pin-spot, and lifts the dead baby in her arms and screams.

Tull-eee-ee!!

Curtain. End of Act One.

Act Two

Scene One

CLARICE sits in a chair, the very archetype of pain and extremity. WILLEM stands next to her, holding her hand.

WILLEM:

I love ya, Leasey ... and it hurts to see ya hurtin' like this ...

CLARICE remains mute. The light broadens; we see SARAH sitting at the table.

SARAH:

Well I guess I best be goin'.

WILLEM:

No no, Sarah, you stay. Leasey wants you here, ain't that right Leasey?

CLARICE makes no response.

SARAH:

I'll make you some tea, Leasey. Don't worry now, the pain gotta come out. Grievin's only natural. It helps take the pain away.

She walks by WILLEM, whispering.

She don't need me here. She needs you, son, she needs your strength. Be strong, strong enough for the both of ya.

SARAH exits. There's silence.

CLARICE:

Where's Tully?

WILLEM:

He'll be at the church, soon, Leasey. They gonna bring 'em to the church.

CLARICE:

Did you tell Reverend Miner what I tol' ya to tell 'em?

WILLEM looks away.

Look it me, Willem. (*Pause.*) I'm talkin' to you. Why I gotta pull teeth?

WILLEM:

I tol' 'em, Leasey, okay? I tol' 'em.

CLARICE:

What he say?

WILLEM:

He said he wants to hold a little memorial service for Tully the day tomorrow.

CLARICE:

(*Angrily.*) Now that ain't what I'm talkin' about! That ain't what I asked ya to tell 'em! (*Beat.*) Oh! ... (*She starts to break down.*)

I can't take this I can't take this! (*Beat.*) Why I gotta be the one to undertake alla this? Why? ... None of this my fault ... none of it I don't understand ... my baby ...

WILLEM:

Leasey.

CLARICE:

... my baby.

WILLEM:

Leasey please don't cry. Don't cry, I tried—

CLARICE:

(*Yelling.*) Why not?! Why not cry, Willem?! No one else 'round here appears to be mournin'!!

There's a very pregnant pause. CLARICE's demeanour changes.

Oh, Willem, I'm sorry ... I'm so sorry ...

WILLEM:

It's okay. Leasey, it's—

CLARICE:

I was just—

WILLEM:

You know the Reverend wants to help us Leasey, but ... but his hands are tied. And Mister Clancy say there are strict laws about—

CLARICE:

Mister Clancy?! (*Beat.*) Why? ... What he got to do with this? He don't know nuthin' 'bout nuthin'!

WILLEM:

Do it matter, Leasey?! (*He slams his hand down angrily.*) He's from the city!! Now how many times I gotta tell ya?!

CLARICE:

Well why you askin' *him* about Tully? He dunno nothing about Tully. He don't know about ... about ... *us.* He ain't got no business ... you shoulda asked Reverend Miner!

WILLEM:

But it *is* his business. That's what I'm tryin' to tell ya, Leasey. Mister Clancy say it *is* his business.

CLARICE:

Oh, he do?

WILLEM:

He say the city got strict laws against what we're askin' and—

CLARICE:

Laws?! What laws? What kinda laws say a mother can't bury her baby? (*Beat.*) What? What kinda laws?

WILLEM:

He say he got city ordinances-like, ah ... whatcha calls by-laws, and he got the police behind him.

CLARICE:

And where was the police when I was cryin' with Tully dyin' in my arms? Where was they when I needed them? Where was the ambulance?

WILLEM:

Leasey, I think you should lay down.

CLARICE:

I can't lay down no more!! (*Beat.*) We been layin' down for those white bastards all our lives!! All, our, goddamn, tired-ol' lives!! Well no more!! I'm sick!! I'm sick and tired of them games they been playin'!!

WILLEM:

Leasey, please.

CLARICE:

Games I tell ya!! (*Beat.*) They play games and experiment with people's lives. They think they're God he's-self!! Live here! Bury them over there!! Well screw those white bastards and the train they rode in on!! And the train run right through Africville, Willem. Has it stopped? It ain't stopped!!

WILLEM:

Leasey, they say ya have to have a special permit for this. People just can't go round diggin' holes and—

CLARICE:

Permits?! Then we apply.

WILLEM:

Ain't no use they tells me. Just be throwin' good money after bad.

CLARICE stands.

CLARICE:

I don't see no permits for them tractors. And them destroyin' creatures—them life-sucking rats—they got permits?! And them trucks—and yes, Groovey was right. They move the Willises in a garbage truck. They got permits for that? Permits to be movin' people's belongin's in garbage trucks? Don't tell me, Willem! I know! The city uses permits only when it suits the city. And the city don't permit no *niggers*!!

WILLEM:

Leasey the man say you gotta have consecrated ground to bury someone. And there ain't no consecrated ground in Africville.

CLARICE:

(*In disbelief.*) No ... consecrated ... ground? (*Beat.*) No *consecrated ground*?! What is Africville if it ain't consecrated ground, Willem? (*Beat.*) This land been in my family for years, *hundreds a years* ... My ancestors, they consecrated this ground ... the kids laughing and playin' in Kildare Field consecrated it! The funerals, the hymns at the church, consecrated it ... All the baptisms down at the beach, Willem, they consecrated this ground. This is where they lived and died ... where ... where they cried ... where they loved, Willem ... loved. (*Pause.*) Surely ... (*She starts to cry.*) Surely no one, ain't nobody on this-here earth tellin' me Africville ain't no consecrated ground!! Ain't no Mister-Clancy-city-white-man tellin' me. I saw it ... I lived it ... I loved it ... Africville is consecrated ground!!

She collapses, breathlessly, to the chair.

Now ... you go. You hear me? You go run, and ... and tell ...
tell Mister Clancy what I say. Tell him he got it all wrong, cause
there ain't a single lick a land in Africville that ain't
consecrated. You tell 'em that.

WILLEM:

Leasey we gonna bury Tully. Bury him in a city cemetery.

CLARICE:

You listen here!! (*Beat.*) They took my chile away from me
once, Willem ... *once*!! They ain't takin' 'em away ag'in—ya
hear?! Ya hear me?! They ain't layin' a finger on my baby. Ya
hear, Willem?

WILLEM:

Leasey they gonna do what they wanna do and that is that.

CLARICE:

Well they got it all wrong. They ain't layin' a finger on my
baby. You go tell Mister Clancy that. You tell 'em Tully's gonna
be buried in Africville where he belongs and—

WILLEM:

Leasey—I tol' ya, baby—it's too late. It's too late for all that
now. All ya gotta do is look around ya and see that they made
up their minds what they're gonna do with us. They're
demolishin' Africville Leasey—

CLARICE:

No they ain't!! We ain't sellin'!

As WILLEM picks up his gloves to exit, a bulldozer suddenly starts.
Both look to the sound, then WILLEM exits in silence.

SCENE TWO

CLANCY, smoking and waiting, stands next to the well as AUNT
SARAH approaches. She doesn't appear to recognize or notice him
and keeps walking.

CLANCY:

Hi!

SARAH:

Mister.

She keeps walking.

CLANCY:

Miss Aunt Lied? (*Beat.*) It's me, Sonny.

SARAH halts.

SARAH.

Oh my. Sonny ... you look diff'ren'. Like you changed or growed or some-such. How ya been doin'?

CLANCY:

Could be better I'm afraid.

SARAH:

Always can be. You look cold. Ya never did come by for that tea.

CLANCY:

I know ... but I'll be by shortly.

SARAH:

Maybe yes, maybe no ... but let me tell you somethin', Sonny. Ya know, all God's chillin' got a role ta play. Just like in them movies. Some plays bad roles, some plays good roles. Then there's thems in them movies that don't know what kinda role they's playin'. Ever see them movies like that-there, Sonny?

CLANCY shrugs; he chuckles.

CLANCY:

Guess.

SARAH:

Now ain't that sumpin'. (*Pause.*) Well I ... I gotta git I tells us. Bye, Sonny. (*She starts off.*)

CLANCY:

See ya.

SARAH:

(*Halting.*) Say, Sonny?

CLANCY:

Yeah?

SARAH:

Did ya ever git them books from the lie-berry I was tellin' ya about? You know? (*Beat.*) The ones 'bout South Africa?

CLANCY:

No, Miss Aunt Lied. I just didn't have the time.

SARAH:

Too bad. (*Starting off.*) Whole world a knowledge in that there lie-berry. Whole lotta understandin'.

She exits. CLANCY butts out his cigarette and exits.

SCENE THREE

CLARICE lies apparently napping in a chair. WILLEM stands nearby, unaware that her eyes are wide open.

WILLEM:

(*Whispering.*) Leasey? (*She doesn't answer.*) Leasey? (*Pause.*) I just stand here and look up through the window into the stars, ya know, Leasey? (*Pause.*) I kin see ... I kin see before all those twinkling stars that the Big Dipper and Venus be as bright ... as bright as the Star of David, baby ... (*Pause.*) Leasey, I—

CLARICE shifts.

It like ... it like the whole universe out there, just waitin' for us to ... step out into it ... Like, baby, I been thinkin' ... maybe it's time we got outta Africville ... and ... and, well, there ain't hardly no one left here anyways. Everybody's gonna go. I'm thinkin' ... yeah ... maybe we should take the city's offer and sell. People always movin', Leasey. White folks move all the time. Mister Clancy say we can relocate to a good, warm place ... in, ah, Uniacke Square.

CLARICE doesn't stir, but stays perfectly still.

I'm thinkin' ... maybe now's the time to leave. See, the city ain't too happy with all the publicity it's gittin' in the papers and stuff and so ... well, they wanna make a deal with us. They got big plans for this land. They talkin' like a park and maybe some industry and stuff. (*Pause.*) Yeah ... Mister Clancy mentioned a park or sumpin' ... Leasey, I dunno ... don'tcha see what this means for us? ... Now's our chance to get out— get a good price for our land, 'cause the city wants it bad and it don't want no trouble. Know what I mean?

CLARICE doesn't answer.

There ain't nothin' we kin do, Leasey. Can't you see that? If the city wants our land, they're gonna take it and it don't

matter what the nigger wants. Never has, never will ... Leasey,
you listenin' to me? Are you listenin', baby?

CLARICE suddenly turns to him, sound asleep.

SCENE FOUR

*REVEREND MINER is doing some business behind the pulpit as a
dishevelled and drunken CLANCY enters. He takes a swig from a
flask.*

REVEREND MINER:
Oh, Mister Clancy.

CLANCY:
Hello, Reverend ....

REVEREND MINER:
I see you've had your taste of the flask again today, Mister
Clancy. You shouldn't fret yourself. You should simply ask God
why He won't give you licence.

CLANCY:
I have my problems, Reverend, but why are you talking to me
like this? I mean, like in circles? ... What licence? What are
you talking about?

REVEREND MINER:
A *licence* to barter, boy, to buy and sell these people's souls.
'Cause that's what you're trying to do. But see, only God
possesses that phenomenal currency. (*Pause.*) Now lock the
door when ya leave, will ya?

REVEREND MINER starts off.

CLANCY:
Reverend?

REVEREND MINER:
(*Halting.*) Yeah?

CLANCY:
I have to talk to you, Reverend.

REVEREND MINER:
I don't want to talk right now! (*He lowers his voice.*) Yes, even
ministers get tired of talking sometimes.

CLANCY:

But I have—I mean, I just need somebody to talk to.

REVEREND MINER:

I want nothing more to do with this business, Mister Clancy.
Now you sober up, and try and make *your* peace with God.

CLANCY:

No, Reverend it's not about that, or ... (*Lifting his flask.*) even
this. It's about me. I mean, the Lyle boy. Dead ... he's dead.
Circumstances beyond my control. But I thought when I got
in here, I'd be the hero—I mean save the people from these
living conditions. Just look at how they live? Next to a dump
for Godsakes.

REVEREND MINER:

The people were here first, boy, then they moved in their new
tenant; the dump. Then there's the abattoir. Naturally, along
with abattoirs and dumps—right along with them—comes
rats. I mean, don't you understand what's going on here?

CLANCY:

You know Reverend? I did everything a good boy—a good
little white boy from the affluent end of town—is supposed to
do. I ... I went to the right schools, the right church. I ... I
cultivated the right friends. My folks have money—guess you
never guessed that, hunh? (*He chuckles; contemplates.*) But I
realize now that I never got this job because they saw some
brilliance in me, or any special aptitude. I got this job because
I'm William Clancy's boy—and you better believe it. The party
that sits on the government side owes my father some favours.
Big, political favours and I'm my father's payback. None of the
other bastards downtown would dirty their hands with this,
you know. By hiring me they killed two birds with one stone,
didn't they? I mean they paid off what they owed my father
and got rid of the Negroes at the same time.

    CLANCY stands.

I just want you to know, Reverend, I want you to know, for the
record: I never had anything to do with people being moved
in garbage trucks! I didn't make that decision. In fact I tried
my best to make sure everyone here would be treated with
respect ... dignity. And that baby? My God, Reverend, that
should have never happened. I ... when I took this job I

thought I could do good. I thought the city was on the up-and-up. But ... Reverend, I'm so sorry. So sorry.

REVEREND MINER:
Tully's death wasn't your fault

CLANCY:
And I'm sorry about the church ...

The REVEREND is taken aback for a few moments.

REVEREND MINER:
What?! They're going to tear down the church?!

CLANCY:
It was after your request to bury the baby. Some members were against the burial. They felt it would encourage—

REVEREND MINER:
Tear down my church?!

CLANCY:
—it would encourage an attachment to this place long after the people were gone. Then, an alderman said if we allow one there would be many more. He felt that allowing the burials in Africville would cause some problems—now, and in the future. Then the next thing I know, someone asks why they should keep the church in Africville. I reminded them of our commitment to you. Some supported me ... but the majority voted to get rid of the church too. I thought you—

REVEREND MINER:
Tear down the church?! What—in God's name—are those imbeciles thinking?! Do they not know, that this church is the very badge of identification for my people?! Do they not know that this is the very cement that holds my people together?! Do they not know that this church is the very soul of ... of Africville itself?!

CLANCY:
Reverend Min—

REVEREND MINER:
Of course they know! (*Beat.*) And that's the very reason why they're tearing, it, down! (*Beat.*) Because if you divide—you conquer. Those e-vil ... gen-it-tal-cutting, bastards!!

There's a long pause.

CLANCY:

> (*Deliberate and even.*) They need Africville 'cause they need
> more harbour frontage! They need Africville so they can build
> a new bridge—approach ramps. Reverend, if they allow
> people to be buried on the site, I mean around the church, it
> would create problems. I mean, it's just not this baby so much.
> It would be all the people of Africville and the generations to
> come. They don't want people seeing a gravesite.

REVEREND MINER:

> Then if they don't want those graves, and if they don't want
> this so-called shantytown, why don't they fix up Africville like
> they did every other community?! Surely it's costing them
> more money to build that Uniacke Square than it would cost
> to fix up Africville!! My people have been asking for their help
> for centuries!! (*Beat.*) For centuries!!

CLANCY:

> Reverend Miner, I—

REVEREND MINER:

> Damn them!! And damn you Mister Clancy!!

> *There's an eerie silence as REVEREND MINER walks to the pulpit.*

CLANCY:

> I don't like this any more than you do, Reverend. But what
> choice do we have? Unless both me and you do what the city
> says, they'll expropriate all the land and give everybody five
> hundred dollars as was the initial plan. And there would be no
> church here or anywhere else. Listen, Reverend, as hard as it
> is, we must complete this plan before the city's deadline. They
> promised me they will rebuild your church at a new site. You
> will have your church.

REVEREND MINER:

> Do you really think they would desecrate a church just to build
> it up again?! This is not part of their, brilliant and evilly,
> executed plan ...

CLANCY:

> (*Angrily.*) Reverend Miner I'm so sick of this!! All this
> subterfuge!! All this lying—this explaining and re-explaining.
> All this deal-making!! Look what it's turning me into!! Look
> what it's doing to you!!

REVEREND MINER:

Don't pity me, Mister Clancy. My heart goes out to you and your city. Now! (*Beat.*) You've had your first taste of power— your first taste of the inhumanity and insensitivity of your system. And you're wondering if it's really you, you're wondering if this is what you wanna be for the rest of your life. You're looking at yourself and you don't like what you see. Do you? That's why you drink.

CLANCY:

Let's just get these last people signed. Get your new church. At least with me and you here, there's still a chance.

REVEREND MINER:

A chance? A chance for what?

CLANCY:

A chance for the church. A chance for human dignity.

REVEREND MINER:

There's no chance for anything now, Mister Clancy. Can't you see? There's no chance for anything now.

There's a very pregnant pause between them, then CLANCY collects his things and exits. The REVEREND simply stands there.

My God ... Why? ... Why have You forsaken me? ... Why? ... Why have You let me down in my time of time of trouble? ... Why? ... why have You chosen me to be strong when everywhere I turn I gaze into the omnipotent eye of adversity?! ... *Why have You failed me?!*

With Bible in hand, he slumps defeatedly into a pew as the bulldozers start again.

In the face of this You give me words?! In the face of metal and bristling machine?! ... (*Pause.*) ... You, give, me, words ... (*He stands.*) I cannot stand before the gluttonous mouth of a bulldozer and fight with ... with words!! (*Pause.*) And my people ... my flock ... they line up behind me ... seeking solace and, and wisdom and strength ... and yet I fail ... I fail ... I may as well lead them to your abattoir over there and prepare them for Your forthcoming slaughter!! ... Why?! ... Why have You forsaken me in my time of need?!

Long pause; he lowers his voice.

Upon this Earth I have served Thee. I have served Thee faithfully. Truthfully. My mouth has sung nothing but Your praises. What is my reward? ... A displaced people, a dead baby and a church to be bulldozed. And when I call on You, You give me impotent words?!

He flings the Bible to the floor.

I, need, a, miracle!!

Pause.

I ... need ... a ... miracle.

Slowly he re-approaches the pulpit.

"Fret not thyself because of evildoers, neither be thou envious against workers of iniquity ..." those are Your words. "For they shall be cut down like the grass, and wither as the green herb ..." those are Your words ... and I have been nothing, nothing but Your mouthpiece. I ... do ... not ... need ... Your ... words!!

He glances to the Bible and retrieves it from the floor and kisses it.

"Thou wilt keep him in perfect peace, whose mind is stayed on Thee ... because he trusteth in me ..." those are Your words ... And my God ... my heavenly Father ... I trust ... I trust ...

Blackout.

SCENE FIVE

CLARICE is dressing in black, gathering her clothes.

CLARICE:

I ain't worn these clothes since Momma died, know that, Sarah? Still fits though, don't it?

SARAH:

Oh sure it do. Sure it do. (*Pause.*) Leasey, you sure you don't want me to come with you?

CLARICE:

No, it's somethin' ... somethin' I gotta do ...

SARAH:

Okay. I just ...

CLARICE starts to break down. SARAH embraces her.

Oh, Leasey ... Leasey Leasey. It be okay, okay? I promise. It be okay ...

CLARICE:

But how? (*Pause.*) How? ... (*Crying.*) Tully Tully-Tully-Tully ...

SARAH:

You got to be strong, girl. We the ones that gotta be strong. Oh yes, we bring 'em into the worl', but we gotta be strong enough to take 'em out of the worl' too. Strong ... strong.

CLARICE:

But ... but ... (*Breaking down.*) I'm tryin' ... I'm tryin' so hard, so hard, Aunt Sarah ... but it's so hard!

SARAH:

I knows. I knows, but ... but this what yer granddaddy and yer grandmomma done for you, and yer momma and poppa, too. You gotta be strong. They taught ya how to be strong.

Silently, CLARICE puts on her veil and goes towards the door, where she pauses.

CLARICE:

I'll be back later.

SARAH:

Yes. You gotta have some of that Blueberry Duff I made for ya. It good ya know.

CLARICE:

(*Smiling through her tears.*) Yeah, I know. (*She embraces SARAH.*) 'Lease it ain't no turnip greens!

They laugh awkwardly, then CLARICE leaves as the kettle boils. SARAH goes about the business of making her tea for a few moments, when GROOVEY appears in the door, suitcase in hand. Unseen by SARAH, she drops the suitcase, and simply stands there. SARAH finishes her tea, and as she turns, sees GROOVEY.

SARAH:

Jesus!! Groovey ya plumb up and startled me! Whatcha doin' just standing there?!

With a rag she's now wiping up tea.

Groovey? Now I raised a lotta babies and I gotta revert to a momma's old standby: "In or out! In or out!" (*She chuckles.*)

SARAH becomes concerned as GROOVEY continues to stand.

Groovey, you all right, baby? You okay? Come in. Sit down.
Come on, honey ...

GROOVEY:

No, Aunt Sarah-girl, Groovey not comin' in, Groovey goin' de
udder way ...

SARAH:

What? My Gawd, what be wrong wif you, Groovey? I mean—

GROOVEY:

Groovey's leavin', Aunt Sarah. Goin'.

SARAH:

On a vacation?! Never thought I'd see the day when Groovey
Peters got tired of her men-friends! (*She chuckles.*)

GROOVEY:

No vacations, no day-trips, I'm tellin' ya girl, Groovey Peters is
leavin' Africville.

SARAH:

Whatever for?

GROOVEY:

"Whatever for"?! Aunt Sarah 'ave you been watching da
goings-on 'round dis place lately?! You ain't seen?! (*Pause; she
lowers her voice.*) Groovey Peters been told. Groovey Peters
knows when Groovey Peters ain't wanted.

SARAH:

You been told? Told what?

GROOVEY:

I got my notice, Aunt Sarah. Groovey Peters is gone, ya hear?

SARAH:

Gone where? What notice? Girl, what are ya talkin' about?

GROOVEY:

Da man done tol' me: "Groovey Peters you must vacate said
properties by ..."—all dat white bullshit, you know? (*She
chuckles.*) Only ones dat don't know it is dem! I appeal to de
man. I dun tings. I mean, for ... "my friend." Me beg—me
plead. Groovey plead for all of Africville, but he drop me like
Groovey fulla polio. Like Groovey don't have no never-minds.
(*Pause.*) Me taught ... (*She starts to cry.*) Groovey taught dis
time it be different for Groovey. He gonna git a divorce and
marry I. (*Beat.*) Groovey actually believed, Aunt Sarah!! (*She

84

cries, but regains her composure.) Well!! (*Beat.*) Groovey ain't no
believer no mores. Groovey goin' back to Montreal where da
people are real and where ya know ya ain't no "*Nay-gro.*"
Where yei a just a plain "nigger." Where dey take advantage of
ya (*Pause.*) but dey kiss ya first, Aunt Sarah!! 'Lease dey kiss ya
first.

SARAH:
Now Groovey.

GROOVEY:
Here? (*Beat.*) Here Aunt Sarah?! (*Beat.*) Groovey just don't
want to see anymore carnage, 'cause that what it be—*carnage*!!

SARAH:
Don't say that.

GROOVEY:
Why not? It be the truth! I see people move in garbage trucks!
Why you yoursel' say it be like South Africa!

SARAH:
You thought he was gonna marry ya? You really thought that
he was gonna marry ya? Girlll ...

GROOVEY:
Groovey let her guard down. Me taught ... me taught me
politician was real. But Groovey knows now—Aunt Sarah: dere
ain't nuthin' in dis worl' dat's white and real. Ya gotta spread
de dark gravy over de white rice before it palatable.

SARAH:
Groovey!

GROOVEY:
Groovey is tired. Nuthin' but lies lies lies lies lies and more of
dem lies. (*Offstage, we hear a car horn.*) My cab!

SARAH:
Let 'em wait! They make us wait, don't they? I'm surprised it
even come to Africville.

The car toots.

GROOVEY:
You know Aunt Sarah ... (*She chuckles.*) When de cabs do
come to Africville dey always so very anxious to get out!

85

SARAH:
Well I'm goin' too, honey. I'm movin' too. Mister Clancy and all his friends dun seen to that.

GROOVEY:
Whatcha you tink Clarice might do wid all dis, Aunt Sarah?

SARAH:
Clarice gotta realize that Africville's over. Over, baby.

The bulldozers start, then, we hear another "beep-beep."

GROOVEY:
Groovey got to git her train, Aunt Sarah. My Grooveytrain come in.

They embrace.

SARAH:
You write or call now.

GROOVEY:
I will.

SARAH:
'Cause you know where ever Sarah Lied be, she gotta phone.

GROOVEY:
All right, Aunt Sarah. Groovey Peters gonna miss ya.

SARAH:
Oh, go on now. Ya gotta run to yer destiny, Groovey. I ... *think* that's what they calls it ... yeah ... destiny ...

GROOVEY:
You tink dis is Groovey's destiny, Aunt Sarah? Oh no, dis just be dere rendition of Groovey's destiny. And dey all playin' da wrong tune.

GROOVEY exits to porch, picks up her bag, waves, then exits.

SCENE SIX

WILLEM sits alone in a pew of the church. We hear a door shut, and silently CLANCY appears and sits behind him.

CLANCY:
Willem?

He still doesn't stir.

Willem Lyle?

WILLEM wipes his eyes and glances behind.

Maybe this is the wrong time. I can come back.

WILLEM:

No, no, come in, Mister Clancy. God's house is open to all.

CLANCY:

You're the deacon here, right?

WILLEM:

Nope. The choirmaster.

CLANCY:

I see. Well ... I brought along that agreement we were talking
about the other day, remember?

WILLEM nods affirmatively.

This won't take long.

WILLEM:

Sure. (*Pause.*) You see Mister Clancy, this place took our baby
and we just wanna ... we just wanna git out as quick as possible.

CLANCY:

Was Tully your only child, Willem?

WILLEM:

Uh-hunh. Yeah.

CLANCY:

Oh ...

WILLEM:

There's no problem is there, Mister Clancy? No problem ...

CLANCY:

No ... it's just ... well ... I mean ... you do realize the city can't
find you a place in Uniacke Square. I mean ... according to
their criteria ... it's a—

WILLEM:

Why, Mister Clancy?

CLANCY:

Because the complex was made for families.

WILLEM:

But we is a family—me and Leasey.

CLANCY:

No no no. Not according to this, I mean, our, criteria. You see you and your wife are now a childless couple. The city will, however, work to find you a place outside Uniacke Square. Okay? You understand?

WILLEM nods affirmatively.

You're happy with your assessment? You're sure you understand what I'm saying?

WILLEM:

Yes. I do.

CLANCY hands WILLEM his pen and the Quit Claim Deed. WILLEM doesn't take it and CLANCY retreats. Then he re-offers it. WILLEM takes it and CLANCY leans his attaché case forward so WILLEM can sign on it. CLANCY takes the deed, gives WILLEM a copy, and silently leaves. WILLEM also exits. He walks to another part of the stage, where CLARICE stands.

SCENE SEVEN

CLARICE is standing in the middle of field. She's deep in thought and vacantly staring off. WILLEM enters.

WILLEM:

(*Softly.*) Leasey!

CLARICE:

(*Gesturing.*) Look, Willem ...

WILLEM:

What?

CLARICE:

I kin feel 'em, Willem. Just like it was yesterday, I kin feel 'em.

WILLEM:

Baby? It's cold out here, too cold to be doin' this. Why don't we—

CLARICE:

This be right where my grandmomma and granddaddy on Momma's side lived. Right near this spot, well ... just over there. We had the closest house to the well.

WILLEM:
(*Weakly.*) Leasey?

CLARICE:
Why you practically standin' in tho middle a their living room. And Granddaddy built their place with his bare hands ... and home-made tools. And ... and ... ya know? I kin feel his spirit, his pride, his love of his land ...

WILLEM:
What happened to the house, baby?

CLARICE:
It ... it burned down ... and Granddaddy died in that field tryin' to save it ... Once again (*Pause.*) 'cause once again the fire trucks came late to Africville. They was always late, real late, and I guess Granddaddy breathed in too much smoke. He died right in Momma's arms he did. Right there in that-there field ... much like ... much like ... much like my Tully did in mine.

WILLEM:
Baby, I never knew—

CLARICE:
All the men folk pitched in and built Momma a new house. The house we livin' in now, and Willem?

WILLEM:
What, baby?

CLARICE:
This is where Tully's gonna be buried. There ain't no one gonna—

WILLEM:
Leasey—

CLARICE:
No I tell you! Tully's gonna be buried right here near us ... where he ain't never gonna be alone ...

> *She throws off WILLEM's arm and bolts. She goes to the church, where CLANCY is sitting.*

WILLEM:
Leasey!!

CLANCY is sitting in a pew in the church. CLARICE enters. He stands.

CLANCY:

May I help you?

CLARICE ignores him.

Haven't we already—

CLARICE:

I've come to talk to Reverend Miner.

CLANCY:

He'll be back in a moment. Are you sure there isn't something I—

CLARICE:

I want to speak to Reverend Miner I said!

They retreat to pews, CLANCY in front, CLARICE angrily eyeing his back. Momentarily the REVEREND enters.

REVEREND MINER:

Clarice! Why I didn't expect—

CLARICE:

In the church, Reverend?! You lettin' this man conduct his business in the church?

REVEREND MINER:

God's house is open to all, sister, you know that.

CLARICE:

Even to the ones that wanna destroy it?!

REVEREND MINER:

(*Clearing his voice.*) Clarice. This is Mister Clancy. Why don't we sit down?

She takes the REVEREND aside.

CLARICE:

Tully got to be buried in Africville, Reverend.

CLANCY:

Excuse me for interrupting—

CLARICE:

No excuse! I ain't here to talk to you. (*Pause. To REVEREND MINER.*) Now Tully's gonna be buried here, Reverend. In Africville where he belong,

REVEREND MINER:

Clarice, do you know why we—

CLANCY:

Excuse me Reverend, but Mrs. Lyle—

CLARICE:

Save it!! Just save it!! (*Beat.*) You desecratin' everything you touch!

CLANCY:

I'm sorry. I'm very very sorry, Ma'am. Look Mrs. Lyle I do empathize with your situation, but the facts are clear—

CLARICE:

You should be sorry!! (*Beat. Emotionally.*) 'Cause you took my baby away from me, Mister Clancy!! I ain't got no baby no more, *'cause you killed 'em*!!

CLANCY:

We did not kill your child, Mrs. Lyle, we—

CLARICE:

Oh yes you did! Killed 'em the day you built that dump on our doorstep. Black, proud people, living right here, and your city comes along and builds a home for rats. But you ain't happy yet, are ya? You ain't happy till ya feed the helpless black babies to 'em!!

Again CLANCY pauses.

CLANCY:

Mrs. Lyle ... look, I'm sorry. I truly am sorry about the loss of your child and the living conditions you endured. But I must remind you, the city, under no circumstances, will agree to consecrate any land in Africville. Do you understand me? Under no circumstances.

CLARICE chuckles, actually chuckles.

CLARICE:

You know Mister Clancy, I like you.

CLANCY:

Thank you.

CLARICE:

But you so young for this job.

CLANCY:

I've heard that so many times, Mrs. Lyle.

CLARICE:

But lemme ask you somethin'.

CLANCY:

What might that be?

CLARICE:

Why they send a *boy* to do a *man's* job?! 'Cause I ain't acceptin' no apologies for Tully from a boy! Send me a white man! You hear me?! You Goddamn well send me a white man! Make him apologize! (*Pause.*) Good day to you Reverend.

CLARICE starts off.

CLANCY:

Mrs. Lyle, may I please ask you one last question.

CLARICE:

No. I got no more to say to you!

CLANCY:

Just one more question? ... Please?

She halts.

CLARICE:

What is it?!

CLANCY:

If you feel so strongly about this place, why'd you agree to sell your land?

She turns to him.

CLARICE:

Whaa—? (*To REVEREND MINER.*) What ... is ... he ... is ... he ... crazy?

CLANCY lifts a piece of paper and hands it to her.

CLANCY:

You do recognize your husband's signature? Don't you? On this Quit Claim Deed?

CLARICE gasps in shock and runs off.

SCENE NINE

*WILLEM sits at table peacefully, sipping coffee and reading the
newspapers. We hear a door slam and CLARICE appears. She's
holding the Quit Claim Deed.*

WILLEM:

Leasey! Groovey's back for the funeral!

CLARICE:

You! ... You black bastard!! You ungrateful sonofabitch!!

WILLEM:

It ... (*Standing.*) it was the best thing. The best thing for us,
Leasey. We kin get a place of our own, start a new life—just
you and me. Leasey ... we ... we been working. Workin' hard
baby, and—and we deserve better than this. There's nothing
wrong with wanting something better. What's wrong with wanting something better? Why can't we have the same things as
the white man?

CLARICE:

'Cause they're lyin'!! (*Beat.*) They don't let niggers have them
things, Willem!! Mister Clancy—all of 'em! They're lyin' to
us!! Can't you understand that?! (*Beat.*) Why can't you
understand that?!

WILLEM:

This place killed our son!! It killed Tully—you want us to die,
too? What is it Leasey, what is it about this place?! This is
nothin' but a tired ol' shack with rats about the doors!!

CLARICE:

Did you sign it on his casket?

WILLEM:

What?

CLARICE:

These papers?! You sign 'em on Tully's casket?!

WILLEM:

I'd have signed them on his *grave*, and so woulda you! But you
ain't thinkin' right, Leasey. I would sign anything to get out of
here!

He goes to hug her and she responds; lifeless.

I did it for us ... I wanted the best ... for us ... Leasey (*Pause.*)
I love you, Leasey ... I love you so much ...

CLARICE:

> (*Weakly.*) Willem?

>> *No reply.*

> Willem?

WILLEM:

> What baby?

CLARICE:

> Willem ... I ... I don't want you here, no more. I ... Willem ...
> I—

WILLEM:

> Leasey—what're ya sayin'?

CLARICE:

> I want you to leave ... to go ...

>> *WILLEM leaves as CLARICE slumps into the couch in a mass of
>> tears. The lights fade, then come up on the church.*

SCENE TEN

> *The church. JIMMY enters carrying the coffin and places it in
> front of the pulpit. He pays his respects and sits in a pew. SARAH
> and GROOVEY enter next. They pay their respects, then SARAH sits
> in the front pew, GROOVEY behind. Next comes CLARICE, who
> breaks down horribly in front of the coffin. SARAH goes and
> consoles her and helps her into the pew as REVEREND MINER takes
> the pulpit.*

REVEREND MINER:

> Now let us pray ...

>> *CLARICE glances behind occasionally, looking for WILLEM.*

Our Heavenly Father, we ask that You give us Your blessing,
Lord. Now let us pray. Lord this child unable to speak, was
known and loved by all who ever held him. Lord please grant
him a place at Your side, in Your Eternal Kingdom. He was
born of Your flesh, dear Lord. He was delivered of Your blood.
He was foreseen to grow into a man who would do good and

great things in Your name. But the longevity of his life was not in Your will, and You called him home. Oh, God, there are many who do not understand. Many who grieve at this close, but Your will is omnipotent and Your reasons are always sound. The Lord works in mysterious ways for His wonders to unfold. He guideth us through the valley of our fears into the place of Eternal peace. He has brought us out of a horrible pit, out of the mirey clay, and set our feet upon a rock, and established our commission. Oh, Lord, Your truth will deliver us.

> *WILLEM enters and starts towards CLARICE, but stops. He stands in the aisle.*

Blessed is the man that make the Lord his trust, and respect not the proud, nor such as turn the lies of the malicious. For even though we walk through the valley of death, we shall fear no evil ... and he shall judge the world in righteousness ... and he shall minister judgement in righteousness, oh, Lord. Amen.

JIMMY, SARAH, GROOVEY, CLARICE, and WILLEM:
(*Together.*) Amen!!

REVEREND MINER:
Let us now turn to—

> *WILLEM interrupts, singing a hymn a cappella. He walks to the casket and lifts it. Still singing, he exits and places it on the soil of Africville. All follow him as he exits. CLANCY stands off in the distance as CLARICE and WILLEM bend over the casket, lifting the soil and pouring it over the coffin. Finally, REVEREND MINER lifts soil and pours it over the coffin, while saying the following.*

Out of the mouths of babes and sucklings hast Thou ordained strength, oh Lord, because of thine enemies. When mine enemies are turned back, they shall fall and perish at Thy presence. And he shall judge the world in righteousness, he shall minister judgement to the people in righteousness, oh Lord. Tully Lyle. The firstborn of Clarice Lyle née Smith and Willem Lyle. A descendant of Africville was born on August 5, 1965, and passed away on October 1st, 1965. His short life received the blessing of the Lord. I do consecrate this holy (*CLANCY crosses himself*) and sacred ground and do bless the small soul that lives herein to eternal and everlasting life in the name of Jesus Christ Our Lord. Amen.

The cast is now back-lit, in silhouette, by the cut-out houses. One by one the light on each of the houses dies. One final light pauses on the church, then it too is extinguished.

Blackout. The end.